Suffering and the Beneficent Community

SUNY Series in Ethical Theory

Robert B. Louden, Editor

Recent years have seen a proliferation of work in applied and professional ethics. At the same time, however, serious questions have been raised concerning the very status of morality in contemporary culture and the future of moral theory efforts. Volumes within the SUNY Press Ethical Theory series address the present need for sustained investigations into basic philosophical questions about ethics.

Suffering and the Beneficent Community

Beyond Libertarianism

Erich H. Loewy

Foreword by David C. Thomasma

State University of New York Press

Published by
State University of New York Press, Albany

For information, address State University of New York
Press, State University Plaza, Albany, N.Y., 12246

Production by M. R. Mulholland
Marketing by Fran Keneston

Library of Congress Cataloging in Publication Data

Loewy, Erich H.
    Suffering and the beneficent community : beyond libertarianism /
Erich H. Loewy.
        p.    cm. — (SUNY series in ethical theory)
    Includes bibliographical references and index.
    ISBN 0-7914-0745-4 (alk. paper). — ISBN 0-7914-0746-2 (pbk. :
alk. paper)
    1. Suffering—Moral and ethical aspects. 2. Ethics.
3. Libertarianism. 4. Consequentialism (Ethics) I. Title.
II. Series.
BJ1409.L64 1991
171'.7—dc20                                                                90-46087
                                                                                    CIP

10 9 8 7 6 5 4 3 2 1

*This book is written in memory of my father
whose thoughts and daily life were its inspiration.*

# Contents

# Contents

# Foreword

There has always been a troubled relationship between physicians and government, between healers and society, between the fantastically singular focus of medicine on an individual and the overall good of the community. Today increasing demand for services offered by modern, technological medicine, increasing costs, social parsimony, and ever more complex requirements on physicians create what Adam Linton, M.D., aptly called "disputes that are visible, political, and emotional."[1] There is no doubt that such disputes will continue now and in the immediate future. They bring immense harm to society, to the profession, and to individual patients.

This troubled relationship has been a source of creativity about the nature of society as well. This is so because the "trouble" exists within the discipline and practice of medicine itself. There is a creative tension in medicine. The goals of medicine and health care include both individualization of care for persons, and concerns about the common weal, its health and its best interests. Indeed, the goals of medical practice also include the physician's own self-interests which have traditionally been in need of balance with the needs of individual patients and the needs of society.[2]

This is to say that physicians must engage in practical justice, righting imbalanced relationships, aiming to return bodies, persons, the profession, their own consciences, and societies to their rightful places.[3] Such efforts are at the core of the discipline. Perhaps that is why many physicians and children of physicians have contributed so much to our conceptions of society and to theories of justice. Justice can only prevail when the proper climate of respect and tolerance can be nurtured and established. Right relationships take place when mutually respectful dialogue occurs, when both individuality and communality in human nature and in human society is affirmed. Physicians, familiar with the practical and the theoretical features of these concerns, are strategically placed to render conceptual help to the rest of us.

Erich Loewy joins a long list of physicians who have written about the nature of human society such as John Locke, and more recently, physicians with such diverse views as Bruno Bettelheim and H. Tristram Engelhardt, Jr. Over the years, Erich Loewy has, like myself, wondered out loud why physicians have turned their minds to the nature of society more often than other professionals.

Perhaps the basic reason is hinted at in Professor Loewy's title: Suffering. Empathetic physicians understand human suffering in a way that few of the professionals can. Suffering creates imbalances that must be righted, not only within the person but also in society itself. A suffering being is an individual whose personhood is threatened. The person may dissolve into an ego and a body that has betrayed that person.[4] One young woman who recently died after a six year battle with ovarian cancer stated unequivocally that not only was she angry with her body as it relapsed into the disease each summer, ruining her vacations throughout high school and into college, but also she was angry with other individuals who were healthy and could pursue normal lives.[5] Thus, an individual who suffers also suffers assaults on their interpersonal and social relations.

So the community becomes involved as well. The second hint also appears in Loewy's title, "the beneficent community." No one can be healed from a disease without reinsertion, somehow, into the community through care. Erich Loewy argues that the morally significant feature of any being is its capacity to suffer. This capacity grounds obligations of beneficence and justice on the part of the community. And this insight functions as the basis for his critique of Libertarianism as a social theory of justice.

Loewy underpins this argument by urging us to consider that fundamental needs and wants of individuals are part of human biology. Not that these fundamental values are reducible to such biological substrata, but rather, he holds that the biological substrate sets the framework for the possible. It is the condition of possibility of both establishing and achieving our deepest desires. Given this reasoning about the capacity to suffer, for example, Loewy argues that when illness happens to an individual in the community it does so because the community has set the social framework both for what illness is and what constitutes it. Yet nothing in the social framework determines the biological basis of the illness. Thus the individual precedes the community.

At the level of the biological substrate, emotion and compassion give rise to caring. Thus the requirement to be just and healing toward one another is not one of social contract, but of fundamental biological ordering. Primitive beings are endowed with an innate sense of pity. For Loewy, unlike for Rousseau, this is taken as the root of the moral impulse. The beneficent community is born.

How is that community developed? The capacity to suffer, the vulnerability with respect to suffering, confers on all animals (not just human beings) with that capacity a prima facie right not to be caused suffering. Nurturing in order to stave off such suffering is the first act of the community towards the individual, primarily in infancy. Hence for Loewy, autonomy, the gradual growth of self-determination in individuals is grounded in a broader moral commitment of the community, that of beneficence. This is the critical point in the argument, for it represents a wholesale critique of modern Libertarianism. Libertarians seem to ground the nature of the community in the prima facie right of autonomy.

For Loewy, the community not only has an obligation to refrain from harming individuals (nonmaleficence), but an active duty to ameliorate and prevent (as far as possible) the suffering of its members. Thus, if there is a social contract, it is one of nurturing one another to overcome the vulnerability of suffering, not primarily one of protecting autonomy.

Erich Loewy is an original and stimulating thinker. His ideas represent the finest alternative to an increasingly shrill reliance on individualism, autonomy, and self-determination in our thinking about the *polis*. Those who traverse this book will be rewarded with prods to standard ways of thinking about political and moral issues. Not everyone will agree. But all will know they have engaged the mind of a person who passionately cares about animals, human life, the environment, and the common good.

*David C. Thomasma, Ph.D.*
*Loyola University of Chicago Medical Center*

References

1. Adam L. Linton, Editorial: "'Right Relationships' Between Physicians and Government," *Humane Medicine* 6, no. 3 (Summer, 1990, 167-169, quote from 169.

2. Edmund D. Pellegrino and David C. Thomasma, *For the Patient's Good: The Restoration of Beneficence in Health Care* (New York: Oxford University Press, 1989).

3. Edmund D. Pellegrino and David C. Thomasma, *A Philosophical Basis of Medical Practice* (New York: Oxford University Press, 1981), pp. 182-191.

4. Jurrit Bergsma with David C. Thomasma, *Healthcare: Its Psychosocial Dimensions* (Pittsburgh, PA.: Duquesne University Press, 1983).

5. Jennifer Lee Onan, "Cancer Writes End to Jennifer's Story," *Chicago Sun-Times*, July 22, 1990, 6.

# Preface

This book proposes to unify ways of looking at individual and communal morality without submerging one for the sake of the other. Often in our daily lives we believe that we need to choose between personal obligation and communal needs. Such a supposed conflict, while it is particularly apparent in medical ethics, is hardly confined to that field. The problem is an old one. Sophocles' play *Philoctetes*, for example, deals with balancing individual and communal claims. Philoctetes, bitten by a serpent and with a foul and malodorous wound, is marooned on an island because his shipmates and Odysseus no longer can stand either his cries or the foul odour of his festering sore. Years later, Odysseus and the community stand in need of Philoctetes' service: Only he has the weapon needed to overcome Troy. But Philoctetes hesitates. His evident yearning for community struggles with his sense of outrage and is resolved, with the help of Heracles' spirit returned to earth, in the mutual recognition of inseparable mutual needs. Arthur Koestler, in *Darkness at Noon*, poses the same problem but without resolution. Rubashov, although innocent of the charges against him, must die for the party's end, ultimately, the nation's good. And die he does, perhaps to be rehabilitated at a later day when the place of the nation and of the party is more secure. Resolutions, in our world, are not quite as simple as they were for Philoctetes: The spirits of the dead no longer appear to point the way. Instead we are left to fashion our own resolutions and to grope for our own accommodations.

The conflict is evident whenever we think that we may need to levy higher taxes for social needs or when we ponder the use of a costly intervention for an aged patient who stands a small—but only a small—chance of benefitting. If we use the framework of interpersonal obligation (the physician-patient relationship is a particularly useful example) our answer will be quite different than if we approach the problem from a purely communitarian point of view. From a purely communitarian point of view, Philoctetus is obligated to go to Troy and Rubashov is bound to be sacrificed or to willingly sacrifice himself. From an individualistic point of view, Philoctetus is quite right in refusing any help to his countrymen and Rubashov must insist upon his personal innocence. When examining such problems, each framework leads to a quite different answer than does the other. And yet, in the real world, both frames co-exist and both frameworks are applicable. Saying that one will apply the frame of reference appropriate to the problem at hand, begs the question: It is not easy to know which frame of reference is, in fact, appropriate to the problem, yet one must choose.

All too often, we have thrown up our hands and evaded the difficult choices. Several examples from medical ethics may be illustrative.

(1)   I saw an eighty-six-year-old black gentleman in ethics consultation in the ICU. It was winter and he lacked sufficient funds to either eat adequately or to heat his apartment to an acceptable temperature. He had been brought into the emergency room about ten days before, malnourished, with a very low body temperature caused by the low temperature in his apartment, and with pneumonia. While in the emergency department he experienced a cardio-pulmonary arrest, was resuscitated, and was then taken to the ICU. Massive attempts to sustain him were made. When I saw him he was on a ventilator, semicomatose and his prognosis for a return of better brain function, according to the neurologist who was seeing him, was virtually nil. The decision to be made—whether to continue to treat aggressively or to merely make him comfortable and allow him to die—was, unfortunately, not difficult.

The telling point of this case is that tens of thousands of dollars had been expended in supporting this poverty-stricken, undernourished old gentleman and every one was quite willing to continue expending even more resources. This was certainly done in good faith and in the hope that perhaps we could return him to his previous state and, then, of course, send him home: a "home" in which, once again, he could starve, freeze and, ultimately get into the same trouble again. The funds spent on this gentleman once he managed to enter the system could very likely have fed and housed a large number of the poor and cold in our community. If one applies the framework of personal obligation, there is no question: All reasonable efforts were justified until, as was the case here, recovery was no longer a reasonable hope. If, on the other hand, one applies a communitarian framework, diverting resources to the black hole of technological rescue strategies instead of expending them on strategies which could have prevented this problem in many others as well as in this gentleman was clearly unjustified. When, in the course of the consultation, I mentioned this oddity, the answer was that "the one problem had absolutely no bearing on the other."

(2)   In our neonatal units across the nation there are tens of thousands of premature, severely damaged children whose chance for meaningful recovery is virtually nil. I speak here of the tiny baby, born long before its time with underdeveloped lungs and severe brain damage which is, nevertheless, kept alive on a ventilator for long periods of time and at incredible cost. The funds consumed have been widely estimated to be sufficient to give prenatal care to a large number of poor pregnant women not getting such care today. Further, it is known that one of the major causes of prematurity and damage is just such a lack of prenatal care. Again, when one mentions this fact, one is likely to be told that such considerations must not enter into individual decisions. That, indeed, may be the case; but even if it is, that hardly eliminates the problem.

Stark as these illustrations in medical ethics are, such conflicts occur in many other contexts. Emphasizing the individual at the expense of the community would cause us to resist passing many regulatory laws and it would suggest that we cannot tax people to fund social programs. On the other hand, emphasizing the community at the expense of the individual can have equally odd results: Privacy and personal fulfillment become almost irrelevant considerations.

Put another way, this clash is quite typical of the conflict between consequentialist and nonconsequentialist ethics. The consequentialist examines only the consequences and judges an act (or a rule) as "good" or "bad" depending upon the amount of "good" or "bad" such an act or rule entails. The nonconsequentialist supposedly ignores consequences altogether and relies on other insights to judge. The individualism of the one ethic, it is believed, must inevitably clash with the communitarianism of the other. If one reduces morality to one system, then one is, indeed, stuck: A resolution between those who claim to look merely at the consequences and those who claim to ignore consequences altogether is not likely. Individualistic societies are inevitably reductionistic: They want to reduce the "we" to the "I" and re-extract the "we" from a simple arithmetic composite of individual "I's." They want to reduce the community to the individual and ignore the common human interests which ultimately produce solidarity.

It is difficult for people reared in this culture to move from the "I" to the "we." Perhaps, as Larry Churchill so incisively notes, we need not so much to move from as to return to: to return from a starkly individ-

ualist posture to one of realizing ourselves in the embrace of community.[1] Community, after all, is inevitably the place of our historical origin. All of us were born to another person in some sort of human
grouping, were, therefore, born into community and were nurtured
and shaped by it. To say "I" without presupposing "we" is, therefore,
incoherent. But to realize ourselves as individuals in the embrace of
community we need to reinterpret, not abandon, the liberal position.[2]
We need to try to conceptualize the liberal position not only within the
framework of community but necessarily as rooted, originating and
forever nourished and sustained by and in community. When we carry
a pure communitarian position to extremes and either do not allow the
individual to emerge and flourish, or when we crush the individuals
who emerge, we end up with Philoctetes merely used, with Rubashov
callously sacrificed and, ultimately, with the prison community of the
Gulag. A community that sacrifices its members for its own sake violates the very notion of community, a notion which inevitably exists for
the sake of mutual needs. Ultimately such communities perish. When
we deny community, when we see in community merely an entirely
voluntary and fluid association of free individuals, when we claim that
individuals do not emerge from community and, therefore, that they
are not obligated to each other and to community, we end up with individuals free to starve to death in the street. Philoctetus or Rubashov
will allow their communities to perish for their own personal ends
regardless of consequences. And in so doing Philoctetus and Rubashov
also ultimately perish.

The thesis that I will try to support in this book is that personal
freedom and fulfillment not only is necessary for community to flourish
but that personal freedom and fulfillment is not possible outside the
embrace of community. It is community that enables the idea of personal freedom and fulfillment and it is the possibility of such freedom
and fulfillment that helps community to flourish and grow. Without
community, personal freedom and fulfillment are meaningless concepts, and it is the possibility for personal freedom and fulfillment
which produces communal solidarity. Community is the necessary condition of freedom and fulfillment, the soil in which individual life is
rooted and without which it inevitably dies. This undeniably socialist
posture which unabashedly sees personal interests as growing out of
community (rather than seeing community as composed of a fluid
association of individuals) can be upheld if one searches not either for
individual or communal morality but rather sees one in the mirror of
the other. Solidarity occurs when individuals see their personal interests as firmly rooted in community. The framework, rather than being

unidimensional, is a multidimensional dynamic in which personal and communal interests are not in opposition to each other but rather inextricably linked and inevitably enmeshed.

I hope to offer a tentative unifying principle of communal and individual morality and I propose to argue for it in two ways: First, I want to sketch out a theory of ethics grounded in the common capacity to suffer, and second, I want to examine a predominantly beneficence-based viewpoint of community. The roots of such a theory are biosocial. This viewpoint does not attempt to reduce morality to biology, but it is predicated on the belief that we are necessarily biological creatures and we are therefore limited by our biological possibilities. Our social life is necessarily underwritten by inescapable biological factors which produce common needs and common interests. Social life is no more reducible to biology than is ethics: both transcend individual biology and both are enabled by and occur within the embrace of biological factors. A theory of individual morality grounded in the capacity to suffer and a beneficent viewpoint of community are inextricably intermeshed. Individual interests and the possibility of individual fulfillment are defined by community. What is and what is not in my interest depends upon the community in which I live. My needs, desires, and aspirations are incoherent without such a specific community. Individuals grounded in community maintain individual interests and needs; ultimately it is only their grounding in community which can assure their personal fulfillment.

In getting this adventure under way, I shall first examine the nature of suffering. Next, I will briefly review some of the other suggested ways of grounding ethics and then return to suffering as the more fertile starting point. Such a starting point may help reconcile and draw together some of the more classical ways of grounding ethics. I shall suggest that, using the capacity to suffer, one can begin to carve out categories of moral worth and then go on to establish hierarchies within the categories. The way in which hierarchies are established is, necessarily, social: communities make their choices not for all times fur for themselves and they must be ready to adapt, change, and learn by trial and error. Inevitably such considerations lead one to examine the roots of social contract, viewpoints of community structure, and the types of obligations consequent to such a viewpoint. Communal and personal obligations determine the way we look at the nature of needs, at the setting of limits and, eventually, at the problems of resource allocation.

This work is not intended to give final answers. Indeed, one of the underlying premises of this work is that there are, in fact, no final answers. The details of ethics as well as the particulars of communal structure are socially determined and variable over time and place.

## References

1. Churchill LR: Getting from 'I' to 'We'. IN: Homer P, Holstein M, eds) *A Good Old Age?* New York, NY: Simon & Schuster; 1990.

2. Brock D: Health Care, Entitlement and the Elderly: A Liberal Critique of Setting Limits. IN: Homer P, Holstein M, eds) *A Good Old Age?* New York, NY: Simon & Schuster; 1990.

# Acknowledgments

It is impossible to name all the persons who have contributed to this book. First of all, I want to thank the editors of SUNY press for their patient understanding and help. Among those chiefly responsible for bringing this book to fruition David Thomasma who not only suggested that I undertake this adventure but who, at a time when we were driving down the road in his car listening to a thunderous version of the 7th Beethoven suggested the title, stands out. He generously gave of his time to criticize, analyze and nurture so that this work owes a great deal to him. Many of the thoughts dealing with community were developed in conversation with the Danish Philosopher Uffe Juul Jensen whom I was visiting at Aarhus Universitet. Much of the fourth chapter was written in Uffe's home at a broad desk overlooking a peaceful garden and with Uffe's cat Sophus critically observing the work in progress. Above all, I am deeply grateful to my wife. Without her knowledge and understanding of philosophy, without her keeping me at least on the philosophically "straight and narrow" and without the opportunity to debate critical points with her, this work would have been neither begun nor finished.

# Chapter One

# The Nature of Suffering

The capacity to suffer and the desire not to suffer are shared by all sentient beings. It is so basic and fundamental a capacity that we often fail to pay much heed to its importance in ethics. And yet it is this capacity which allows us to differentiate between the act of kicking a ball (judging such an act a morally neutral one and calling it exercise) and the act of kicking a dog or a child (judging the act to be morally wrong and calling it brutality). Dogs and children have experiences and have the capacity to suffer; balls do not. Our capacity to differentiate between the two acts of kicking rests on our capacity to feel compassion with the suffering of entities who we feel share, at least to some degree, such a capacity with us. This book will argue that the capacity to suffer can be used as a universal grounding (even if a rather thin grounding, and one in need of development) for our behavior towards others.

Our relations with each other do not simply involve particular actors actings at a particular time. Our relations with each other are determined by and occur in a community. Individual selves begin in community, and communities, in turn, are constituted of individual selves. The relationship I shall explore is a complicated and interwoven one. Our moral presuppositions when we look at community are critical to the way we ultimately look at justice and rights. These moral presuppositions shape the evolution and determine the solidarity of our community. I shall argue that communities are more than merely a composite of individuals, that communities are more than merely the means by which individual ends can be reached. Since I will use the capacity of all sentient beings to suffer as one of the underpinning conditions of community and argue that communities are shaped by, evolve, and maintain their solidarity by an ongoing search for minimizing the suffering of their individual members, a concept of suffering is basic to the way I shall look at both individual and communal ethics.

## Basic Notions of Suffering

Pain and suffering are felt to be integral parts of living. We speak of them frequently, especially when it comes to thinking about illness and disease. And yet, neither the literature of medicine or the philosophical, sociological, and psychological literature deals with the concept of suffering in any systematic or thorough fashion. The theological literature, on the other hand, tends to deal with the subject in a peculiar way: At times, suffering is seen as punitive, at others as redemptive, and while it still carries a negative connotation, some of the religious literature tends to examine what it apparently views as the more positive aspects of suffering.

Suffering, in many religious traditions, is seen as justified either because it is rewarded, deserved, or redemptive.[1] The suffering of innocents, rewarded by eternal bliss, has been used historically to keep slaves, serfs, and, ultimately, the proletariat in line: With eternal bliss just around the corner, why worry unduly about the here and now? In both religious and secular terms, suffering may be seen as deserved. We see that sort of thing in the day-to-day world when we say that smokers deserve to get lung cancer, drinkers deserve their cirrhosis, and the homosexuals or drug addicts who suffer from AIDS deserve their affliction. In theological terms, sinners may be condemned to hell or be sent to purgatory for a period of redemptive suffering. But, in this work, we shall leave such theological considerations aside. In addition, we shall not consider suffering that has a sufficient number of positive elements known to the sufferer so that it is willingly or perhaps even gladly endured. That is not the suffering of which we speak.

All situations of cognitive existence offer the possibility of suffering.[1] Suffering carries a large number of connotations. The Oxford English Dictionary defines it as "the bearing or undergoing of pain, distress or tribulation." To suffer is to "have something painful inflicted" or "to submit to with pain, distress, or grief." The implication is one of a stimulus that is both disagreeable and protracted. Many events of our daily lives are both disagreeable and protracted; and yet we would hardly claim all of them to be a cause of suffering. So, merely being disagreeable and merely being protracted does not qualify. Suffering, in addition, carries a connotation of allowing something to occur which one might easily stop: the statement in the New Testament (or, at least, the common English translation) "suffer your little children to come onto me" may serve as an example. The implication here is not of something necessarily to be endured but of something to be permitted. That meaning, while it forms a background to our contemporary understanding of the word, is generally not the meaning we give to the term today. Nevertheless, the term carries a large and inevitable baggage of historical significance and, furthermore, has many nuances of contemporary meaning. If one is to use suffering as a unifying concept, then, one needs carefully to lay out what precisely one means by the term and how it is to be used.

Pain and suffering are often equated with each other.[2] Bodily pains (for which the question "where does it hurt" is an appropriate one) and pains of the soul (for which such a question has no clear meaning) are, by that analysis, both describable as pain.[3] But the one (whether it does or does not have a demonstrable organic cause) is experienced as having a definite bodily locus, the other does not. In this book, I shall differentiate between pain and suffering. Such a differentiation may appear to be a form of quibbling; however, I think that it can be demonstrated that there are important anatomical, conceptual, and phenomenological differences which make the distinction worthwhile.

The way the term "suffering" will be used here implies a number of things. Suffering is, first of all, a disagreeable experience and an experience one would wish to avoid. It is true that what causes one person to suffer does not cause suffering in another, so suffering has to be defined on individual terms: When what makes another suffer is painless (or, perhaps even pleasurable) to me, I cannot be said to suffer. When one willingly endures suffering, one does so to serve a larger purpose and not because suffering itself is sought out. In such cases, say when one willingly undergoes protracted chemotherapy or accepts suffering as a means for salvation of a different sort, one does so in the hope of affecting a cure or of gaining salvation. The trial is accepted for a higher integrative purpose, and while it has some of the elements of suffering it is a suffering considerably different than some other. As Frankl has pointed out, suffering no longer is suffering when it finds a meaning.[4] A critical component of suffering is its lack of meaning to the one suffering. "Meaning" here is used in two quite different senses. One sense is that for a negative experience to become suffering it has to be remembered, integrated and understood; without such memory, integration and understanding it remains merely a single or a series of noxious stimuli. On the other hand, when Frankl speaks of "meaning" he is speaking about understood negative sensations which cease to be true suffering when they subserve a person's greater goal and become meaningful. As we shall see when we examine the biological underpinnings of sensation, pain, and suffering, sensation becomes pain when it is perceived in certain ways, and pain can become suffering when it is seen to serve no purpose and, in that sense, to have no meaning.

Understood pain or discomfort, then, is no longer suffering in the same sense as is the same pain or discomfort when its meaning or purpose is not understood. This has profound implications for the understanding of suffering in different situations and by different organisms at different times. Suffering is a supple concept which differs from organism to organism, is variable in degree, and is modulated by associated circumstances.

Suffering, furthermore, is not a purely physical matter. Physical pain, even though it is often associated with and often provokes suffering, is not in itself enough to cause suffering. To suffer, an emotional response to a given situation by a given individual is necessary. Suffering cannot be reduced to pain, nor is pain necessarily equivalent to suffering. Some have felt that experiencing loss is an essential element of suffering whereas it is not necessarily an essential component of pain.[5]

Freud speaks of suffering as entailing the antithesis of the pleasure principle. Suffering, as Freud speaks of it, (although without giving a clear definition) threatens us from three directions. It comes to us (1) "from our own body, which is doomed to decay and dissolution and which cannot even do without pain and anxiety as a warning signal," (2) by threats from the external world "raging against us with overwhelming and merciless forces of destruction," and (3) "from our relations to other men." Freud, rightly or wrongly, thinks that the suffering which may be entailed in our relations with other men may be the worst of all because it is a "gratuitous addition" brought about by another's volition rather than being, in a sense, inevitable.[6] Enduring the pain of terminal cancer may, all things considered, be less important in the suffering of the cancer patient than is the frequent alienation from others.

Suffering is something experienced by an individual.[7] Its existential quality is subjective and peculiar to the individual suffering. A given stimulus at a given time may cause one person to suffer while causing only mild discomfort to another. The same stimulus applied to the same person at different times may provoke suffering at one time and not at another. We suffer in a particular context and we carry to our suffering an emotive baggage of present context as well as of history and a sense of the future.

The importance that meaning or the lack of it plays in differentiating animals from humans is an important issue. Many have argued that animals cannot find meaning because animals lack a history. Others have claimed that Freud's concept of suffering can apply only to humans and cannot be applied to animals. I want to challenge both of these contentions.

If the statement that animals "cannot grasp the problem of meaning" were true, if animals could never find meaning in their pain (a statement I take strong issue with), animals could be said to suffer more rather than less. If none of my pain is understood, then my pain is far more likely to become suffering. Such an argument would have a distinctly strange consequence: If animals cannot find meaning in pain and if, therefore, they are much more likely to suffer, we must be far more concerned with the pain of animals than we need be concerned with an equivalent pain in humans. Pain that is not understood, events which are perceived as a threat because they lack explanation must, if we are to do all we can to avoid suffering, be of special concern to us. It is for this reason that we must have special concern when dealing with the mentally impaired.[8]

The argument that higher animals are incapable of reasoning or of finding meaning cannot be substantiated. Higher animals most certainly show the capacity to act in more than a mere reflex fashion and can be easily shown to reason consequentially. Arguing that their behavior is still merely reflex because it is in response to their innate biology begs the question. The same argument can be made with equal force about humans. Human action is no less in response to innate biology than is that of lower animals. Biology of necessity underpins all actions, but this does not equate animals and humans. The capacity to reason and the resulting capacity to find meaning are evolved capacities and are unlikely to have sprung forth biologically unanticipated in humans. As we shall see, the development of those anatomical structures necessary for reasoning, feeling, and having emotions is (like the development of the cardiovascular or renal system) one which has developed as a result of evolutionary forces. Having a better cardiovascular system (or being able to reason more effectively) is adaptive and has survival value. To claim otherwise is to reason in a creationist fashion.

The claim that animals cannot meet Freud's conditions for suffering likewise cannot be substantiated. Animals have a capacity to reason, even if that capacity is, in general, less than the equivalent capacity in humans. It is the capacity to reason which ultimately underpins Freud's conditions. Without reasoning his conditions cannot even be approached. Animals, just like humans: (1) need pain as a warning signal and have pain due to the "decay and dissolution" of their bodies; (2) are threatened by the external world (especially by mankind); and

(3) have relations with others which can bring them severe grief. Those of us who have watched a dog or a bird grieve for the loss of its mate or of its owner, those who have seen the eyes of a faithful dog beaten by its master cannot well deny this!

Suffering happens not just to individuals but to individuals in community. The nature of suffering (not only how we behave when suffering but also those things which cause us to suffer) is conditioned, and in a very real sense defined, by the community in which it occurs. Examples of this are not rare: a person who is suffering severely in one place or under one circumstance, may not do so or may do so far less in another place or circumstance. The hospice movement rests on that observation. A person may not truly suffer or may suffer far less under similar circumstances in the embrace of a religious (or other close-knit) community than he or she would in another context. Martyrs (religious as well as secular martyrs) joyfully embracing their martyrdom are, historically at least, not rare. The suffering individual and the community in which such suffering occurs cannot be separated. When community supplies solidarity and purpose, suffering is transmuted.[9]

There are many components to the notion of suffering, none of which is alone either necessary or sufficient for the concept. Suffering may, but does not have to, entail hurting, being afraid, not understanding, or loss and it often includes an element of hopelessness as well as a sense of being without power to change the events we fear (or know) will happen.

## Biological Considerations

Pain, in general, is a warning: a biological alarm which counsels us that something is going awry and that, if we can, we had best find out what is wrong and do something about it. It is a crucial biological safety device, something like the idiot lights in my car which flash a warning that ought not to ignore, at least until I investigate its cause. Pain is a protective device, a biologically crucial survival mechanism that is purposively noxious and meant to stimulate behavior leading to escape from the stimulus or situation. Behavior may be very simple (I take a pebble out of my shoe, avoid a blister, and perhaps save myself from a terrible infection) or, in our social setting, very complicated: I get chest pain and seek hospital care. A dog yelps and moves his foot away from a bumble bee, or he comes to his master and lifts his paw to have an injury treated or a splinter removed.

Whatever else pain is, it is something all organisms try to avoid unless a compelling reason to seek it overrides that primitive desire. For example, I may undergo more pain to have coronary surgery after my chest pain causes me to seek admission, and the dog may hold still when his master extracts the splinter or fixes the injury despite the pain that not running away may entail. Suffering does not have quite the same teleological usefulness; it carries with it many more connotations than merely having pain does.

Pain, however, is more than simply a reflex response to a noxious stimulus and moving out of the way. After all, amoebas and worms will show such reflex responses but we hardly attribute pain to them. Our failure to attribute pain may be wrong: It may be that the avoidance behavior of amoebas and worms should be properly seen as pain. However, I believe that one can show that there is more to pain than merely avoidance behavior and that our assumption that amoebas and worms do not feel pain is correct.

Reacting to a stimulus does not necessarily entail conscious perception. Dead fish may jump under the influence of certain stimuli, and patients whose spinal cords are severed and who have no sensations from their waist down will, nevertheless, react (and even react quite violently) to an unfelt hammer tapping their knee. The observation that dead fish jump and persons with spinal cord trans-sections exhibit a knee-jerk is not sufficient reason to conclude that sensation is felt. Such cases demonstrate a dissociation between sensory perception and motor response.

Sensations are felt (appreciated or perceived) when there is a functioning neocortex connected to the area of stimulation by functioning nerve tracts. When either a functioning neocortex is absent or when nerves from the neocortex are absent or nonfunctioning, impulses either cannot be perceived (the neocortex is absent or nonfunctional) or cannot be transmitted (the connection between stimulus and cortex is absent or nonfunctional) and sensation perceived. In both these cases, the motor response may remain unimpaired, severed and separate from the sensation. In biological organisms as we know them, the presence of a functioning neocortex seems to be a necessary condition for sensation to occur. This does not, by any means, reduce pain perception to the neocortex nor claim that some other structure in as yet undiscovered organisms may not serve equally well; it does, however, advance the claim (substantiated by an enormous body of evidence) that in organisms as we know them the neocortex is a necessary condition of pain.

For noxious stimuli to become pain several things are necessary. There is, of course, the initial stimulus extrinsic or intrinsic to the organism, be it a pebble in my shoe or an ache in my stomach. Such a stimulus, may, of course, be neurotic: people may believe that they are having terrible pain when no demonstrable cause can be found. This either means that no organic cause for sensation exists, that we have not been diligent enough in our inquiry, or that our knowledge of pathology is insufficient to allow us to find the true cause. Even when, however, no organic cause truly exists, emotional or psychological factors provide what is, in fact, a stimulus.

Once stimulation from whatever source occurs, connections from the area of stimulation to the place in which the stimulus is perceived must be in place and must be functioning. That is what is lacking in our paraplegic: the stimulus is there, the perceptive organ (the neocortex) is intact and functional, the motor ability to respond is unimpaired but the connections between the stimulus and the perceptive organ are severed. A reflex arc connecting the patella to the muscles of the leg by way of the lower spinal cord mandates a muscular twitch even though no sensation occurs.

In the worm, on the other hand, what primitive neural structures exist are not directed to cognition and merely make of such organisms somewhat more elaborate reflexive creatures. It is, somehow, the neocortex which is involved in translating a stimulus into a patient's pain. The neocortex takes the stimulus and makes of it more than a repetitive series of instances. To perceive a stimulus as ongoing rather than as merely intermittent, to realize that one instance is connected to the instance before it, some memory is essential. Kant calls this "re-cognition": a process of "knowing again."[10] However primitive, memory enables thought by integrating sense perception into itself.

To feel pain, then, requires an external or internal source of stimulation, a structure which receives the stimulus, connections from such a structure to higher centers of perception and ultimately structures which are able to connect instances with each other.

Pain is neither a necessary nor a sufficient condition of suffering even though it is what is most frequently thought about when the term is used.[7,11] It is not a necessary condition because extreme suffering can take place without actual physical pain: the mother watching her child being beaten to death while she stands helplessly by, the wife seeing her husband's agony, or the man seeing his reputation ruined or his work trivialized, are all suffering, sometimes far more profoundly than even those in severe pain. Pain, on the other hand, is not a sufficient condition for suffering: merely having pain does not denote suffering. The young teenager having her ears pierced or the person being tattooed is experiencing pain, but they cannot be said to suffer. The pain is of brief duration, not terribly severe and in pursuit of a desired goal.

Prolonged pain is not necessarily equivalent to suffering, although it gets closer to the mark. Persons with an ingrown toenail or a mild headache ordinarily do not feel that they are suffering. The severity of pain alone does not, by itself, entail the agony of suffering. I may have a very severe but brief pain and looking back at it would laugh to think of it as suffering. A combination of severity and duration comes closer to the mark but is also not entirely sufficient. One may have rather pro- longed and rather severe pain: it is disagreeable, it would, whenever possible, be avoided by most persons but just because it is disagreeable and, if possible to be avoided, it still may not be classifiable as suffering. Other features seem to enter into the equation.

Current sensation has to be, as we have seen, connected with past sensation if a discrete stimulus is to be changed into pain. Suffering, however, entails more. In however primitive a fashion, the capacity to suffer entails an ability to realize the future: I am suffering because a stimulus existed before, exists now and may, for all I know, exist in the future. It is this realization of future which underwrites hope and courage as well as hopelessness and despair. To hope or to loose hope implies a realization of the future. We may suffer but have hope or we may have lost all hope and so suffer more. But to suffer we must realize that there was a yesterday and that there is a tomorrow.

To translate pain into suffering is an even more complex issue than deriving pain. Anatomically it would seem that, beyond a neocor- tex, elaborate frontal lobe connections are needed. It is an old experience that patients with severe pain who undergo frontal lobotomy for "pain relief" will continue to acknowledge their pain but lose the capacity to suffer.[12] When asked, they readily affirm their pain but say that it doesn't really bother them: They are not—and they will readily tell you that they are not—suffering.

There is, however, a lot more than just the frontal lobe involved. Darwin suggested that evolution is as much involved in the formula- tion of emotions as in the development of physical traits.[13] In this cen- tury the fact that the limbic system is intimately connected with emo- tions and somehow involved in suffering has been clearly shown.[14] The limbic system, the thalamus and the hypothalamus "set the emotional background on which man functions intellectually."[15-17] When frontal lobotomy relieves the suffering associated with severe pain, the relief is not simply due to a disconnection of the frontal lobes from the rest of the neocortex. A complicated interruption of pathways between the frontal lobes, the rest of the neocortex, and lower structures associated with emotion occurs. An actual distinction between pain and suffering, apparently underwritten by an elaborate neurological system is a bio- logically very valid one.[18]

Moreover, structure is hardly the whole story. The brain is not merely an elaborately wired electrical sensing device. It is far more. Neuroreceptors and neurotransmitters play a crucial role in the function of the brain. Our emotional responses, including our capacity to suffer, are underwritten by a vastly complex and intricately interrelated system in which many forces play roles. These forces, while perhaps at the highest stage of development in man, did not appear de novo in man, and the ability to feel, think, and, ultimately, to suffer, are certainly present in organisms that have a neocortex and an associated limbic system.

Suffering, no more than thought or feeling, can be reduced to the material things which go to make up neural structures. Our capacity to feel, think, and suffer is far more than that. Neural chemistry and structure, however, forms the necessary substrate allowing the functions of thought, feeling, and suffering. The presence of a functioning neurological system does not equate with thought or feeling but the absence of such a system removes the possibility of function altogether.

## Nonbiological Considerations

Suffering has strong connections to hopelessness and despair. Knowing that my suffering will shortly come to an end, or that it has meaning, may convert the suffering into endurable pain; knowing or believing that my suffering is interminable aggravates it or converts mere pain (sometimes even relatively mild pain) into profound suffering. We suffer when we realize that no chance for improvement exists or, even worse, that things are likely to get worse instead of better. Shattering hope, for example, is a way of causing people to suffer. Despair, while it is generally associated with hopelessness, implies even more: It is a more global phenomenon. I may feel that my condition is hopeless, that I will not recover and that, in the nature of things, I will continue to have pain or even to suffer. But I may, at the same time, find some satisfaction in other things. Despair denotes not only hopelessness in one sphere but hopelessness overall: There will be no improvement, there is no joy and there can be no salvation. It is suffering beyond compare. Hopeless grief (despair) is, as Elizabeth Barrett Browning has pointed out, passionless. It suffers without hope, without options "in everlasting watch and moveless woe." It is alienated and withdrawn: beyond protest or tears.[19] In some religions, despair is the ultimate sin: When we despair we lose all belief in the ultimate goodness and purpose of God. It is an affirmation that we are alone in a hostile and incomprehensible world.

When I have options to my suffering, suffering is greatly reduced. A sense of impotence, a lack of control over my own destiny, aggravates suffering or, sometimes, can convert pain to suffering. If I know that I can stop my pain, if I know, even, that I can end my life, suffering is reduced. Prisoners in Nazi death camps, dehumanized and in despair, often went unprotestingly to the gas chambers. The realization that there was an option, even if only the option of committing suicide, stimulated at first a rash of suicides and not much later revolt: The knowledge that some option exists, however dismal, is preferable to none. Patients riddled with cancer who have the means of suicide at hand likewise have been known to take comfort in their ability to be the masters of their own fate. Their pain persists, their suffering endures but the degree of their suffering is reduced.

Fear is often a very real part of suffering and fear is often connected to some of the other elements such as lack of understanding or powerlessness. We fear what we know will happen but we may fear what we do not understand far more. The human species' ongoing attempt to "explain," in reasonable or what seems at times unreasonable ways, has been and continues to be a very important human activity. We fear what we do not understand and we try to remove this fear by labeling and explaining even when the label does not promote understanding or the explanation defies human reason or experience. Thinking we know is better than knowing we don't.

So far we have seen that in order to convert sensation to suffering, a functioning neocortex with complex neural relationships to other structures connected to the point of perception is necessary. Such a point of perception may be internal or external. I may reflect on past experiences or on missed opportunities and, in consequence, suffer extensively. On the other hand, a sustained and inescapable physical stimulus may condition my suffering. All the elements ultimately concerned with the capacity to suffer are elements which ultimately have to be sorted out and integrated into a functioning neocortex. A functioning neocortex and its complicated skein of interconnections is the necessary but not the only condition for suffering.

Patients with terminal cancer are among the most frequent examples of suffering which spring to mind when the term is used. Examining how such persons suffer can help us begin to understand some of the mechanism of suffering. Pain alone fails to describe what these patients experience. This is at once apparent when one considers that certain neurosurgical procedures may alleviate or, at times even eliminate, suffering while pain continues. Patients with severe pain who have had some of these procedures deny suffering but continue to have pain without, however, complaining about it.

The suffering of terminal cancer patients, then, involves much more than pain. Pain, of course, is a frequent element; but it is pain which may well not be as severe as some other pain, which, under other circumstances, would not cause suffering. Hopelessness enters in and despair may appear. Patients may feel completely out of control and unable to control their own destiny. The social dimension of cancer in our particular society, what we know and don't know about it, the way we historically have looked at it and the way we look at it today, all condition the cancer patient's particular agony. Add to this that medicine, at least in America, deals, for a variety of cultural reasons, very poorly with pain and suffering.[20] The cancer patient whom we often take as the paradigm of suffering, however, is not alone. The ethics of managing pain (and suffering) is a subject which has not been well addressed.[2]

Patients with AIDS suffer, in some ways similarly to terminal cancer patients. Communal attitudes and expectations greatly condition not only the diagnoses physicians make and the explanations they use but likewise the responses patients have towards their physical illness. Anthropologists have shown that certain conditions or circumstances in certain population groups seem to cause little suffering. The particulars of what causes suffering and the way in which persons suffer is socially defined. The way childbirth is viewed socially has much to do with the way that the pain of childbirth is experienced by women. This is readily apparent not only in widely disparate cultures but has changed within our own cultural context in our own lifetimes. In societies in which illegitimate pregnancy is a cause for terrible shame, the parents of the pregnant girl as well as the girl herself may suffer horribly; in societies in which illegitimate pregnancy is an expected occurrence, such parents may look forward to their daughters confinement with joy.

## Community and Suffering

For our purposes, we shall consider that creatures who have the capacity to suffer must have (1) the ability to sense internal or external sense stimuli and (2) an appreciation of past, present, and future as connected. This requires, at however primitive a level, the faculty of thinking and reflecting. A neocortex and an associated limbic system, although not sufficient in themselves as conditions, are, nevertheless and in biological organisms as we know them, necessary conditions so that suffering can take place. Furthermore, suffering is something that happens to individuals and suffering is individually defined; but suffering inevitably is conditioned by the community in which such suffering occurs (even when a hermit suffers, she suffers in the way her community of origin has conditioned her). Suffering, therefore, is a process which has biological and social dimensions inextricably intertwined with each other. To truly understand suffering requires us to understand both the individual and his needs as well as the community in which his suffering occurs.

Suffering is a universal. All sentient beings share a common capacity for suffering even if such suffering is provoked by very different events in one than it is in the other. Furthermore, the intensity of suffering of which an individual or a species is capable may be variable: Not all people and not all creatures can suffer to a like extent. All sentient beings live in community, be it the community of a small family or the community of herds or flocks, and suffering occurs in the embrace of community and is conditioned and modulated by it.

Suffering, in a sense, separates persons from community. Suffering persons tend to withdraw into themselves and to feel alienated from a community going on with its daily lives and tasks while they suffer. When communities ignore those within their embrace who are suffering and when they treat them uncaringly or callously the integrity and solidarity of community is shattered. This is true not only when patients who are in pain are ignored and not given necessary medication to relieve their pain; this is likewise true when communities ignore the basic needs of some of their members whose agony of deprivation remains unattended.

## Suffering and Ethics

The capacity of so-called higher animals not only to feel pain but to suffer has been doubted by some. They will claim that while higher animals will often appear to be suffering, our attribution of that capacity to them is a form of glaring anthropromorphism; an interpretation by us, in our own human terms, of what animal behavior denotes. Since animals cannot inform us that they suffer, so the argument goes, we cannot infer that their behavior denotes suffering merely because it resembles our own behavior when we suffer. Yet higher animals have a neocortex and an associated limbic system, have (although some will even deny this) an undoubted memory and an ability to think, and, in addition, exhibit behavior which most of us associate with suffering. The burden of proof, it seems, rests on those claiming that despite the presence of the anatomical conditions for suffering (a neocortex and limbic system), despite a memory, despite an ability to think, and despite the fact that these animals exhibit, under appropriate circumstances, behavior generally associated with suffering, they do not suffer.

Primitively speaking, to have the capacity to suffer implies that one has the ability to recognize at some conscious rather than reflex level that noxious stimuli are noxious and to go beyond this. I have chosen to attribute ethical importance to the capacity to suffer rather than merely to the capacity to sense pain. To judge whether an organism is or is not sensing pain ultimately depends upon the behavior an organism exhibits when responding to stimuli we consider to be noxious. In the sense of responding to noxious stimuli, amoebas sense pain; but amoebas do not knowingly sense pain or have the capacity to extract suffering from such a sensation. While we do not know this with absolute certainty, evidence for this statement is overwhelming. There are, furthermore, many more ways of injuring a sentient entity than by causing pain. Focusing on pain, rather than on the more global concept of suffering, is too narrow. Saying merely that we should not cause pain to another who can sense pain excludes too many other hurtful actions which we intuitively feel need to be condemned or, at least, explained and justified. I will argue that one has a prima facie obligation not to cause suffering, and that, of course, includes the obligation not to cause pain to all (including higher animal)entities capable of suffering. Since organisms not endowed with the capacity to suffer cannot be conscious of noxious stimulation, I will forgo arguing that one has any direct prima facie obligation to organisms not endowed with this capacity. Further, I will argue that communal values as understood in beneficent communities imply an obligation beyond the prima facie obligation to refrain from causing suffering to others. Obligations, where possible, to ameliorate or prevent the suffering of members of community are likewise binding.

## References

1. Rawlinson MC: The Sense of Suffering. *J Med Phil* 11:39-62, 1986.

2. Edwards RB: Pain and the Ethics of Pain Management. *Soc Sci Med* 18(6):515-23, 1984.

3. Edward RB: *Pleasures and Pains: A Theory of Qualitative Hedonism.* Ithaca, NY: Cornell University Press, 1979.

4. Frankl VE: *Man's Search for Meaning.* New York: Simon Schuster, 1963.

5. Kosskoff YD, Hagg S: The Syndrome of Suffering: A Pragmatic Approach.

*Am J Clin Biofeedback* 4:111-16, 1981.

6. Freud S: *Civilization and Its Discontent*. James Strachey, trans. New York: W. W. Norton, 1961.

7. Cassell EJ: The Nature of Suffering and the Goals of Medicine. *NEJM* 306(11):639-45, 1982.

8. Loewy EH: Treatment Decisions in the Mentally Impaired: Limiting but Not Abandoning Treatment. *NEJM* 317:1465-69, 1987.

9. Reich WT: Speaking of Suffering: A Moral Account of Compassion. *Soundings* 72(1):83-108, 1989.

10. Kant I: *Kritik der Reinen Vernunft*. Baden-Baden: Suhrkamp Verlag, 1988.

11. Cassell EJ: The Relief of Suffering. *Arch Int Med* 143:522-23, 1983.

12. Kosskoff YD, Dennis W, Lazovik D, and Wheeler ET: Psychological Effects of Frontal Lobotomy Performed for the Alleviation of Pain. *Res Publ Assoc Res Nerv Ment Dis* 27:723-52, 1948.

13. Darwin CR: *The Expression of the Emotions in Man and Animals*. New York: D. Appleton & Co., 1873.

14. Herrick CJ: The Function of the Olfactory Parts of the Cerebral Cortex. *Proc Nat Acad Sci* 19:7-14, 1933.

15. Papex JW: A Proposed Mechanism of Emotion. *Arch Neurol Psychiat* 38(4):724-43, 1937.

16. Cobb S: *Emotions and Clinical Medicine*. New York: W. W. Norton & Co., 1950.

17. Foltz, EL and White LE, Jr.: Affective Disorders Involving Pain. In Julian R. Youmans, ed., *Neurological Surgery* 2nd ed., vol. 6. Philadelphia: W. B. Saunders Company, 1982. p. 3727-38.

18. Watts JW, Freeman W: Frontal Lobotomy in the Treatment of Unbearable Pain. *J Int Coll Surg* 27:715-22, 1946.

19. Browning EB: Grief. In *The Pocket Book of Poetry*. M. E. Speare, ed. New York: Pocket Books, 1943.

20. Wanzer SH, Federman DD, Adelstein SJ, et al.: The Physician's Responsibility towards Hopelessly Ill Patients: A Second Look. *NEJM* 320:844-49, 1989.

# Chapter Two

# Grounding Ethics

Whatever we do in life, some ground for thinking or acting in certain ways underwrites the judgments we make. Even those who claim to be acting without such firm footing unwittingly are compelled to do otherwise. A framework is inevitable whenever a decision needs to be made. Acting capriciously and without a basis or framework is underwritten by the premise that acting capriciously is what we want to do.

All of our judgments and decisions ultimately must be grounded in nonverifiable assumptions. The fundamentalist may deny this; but the fundamentalist grounds her judgments and decisions either in a religious belief based on revealed truth or, at least, on the assumption that "somewhere out there" truth exists and that we, in the human condition, can know it. Ultimately, or at least up to this point in time, absolute verification eludes man.

At the extreme of this point of view, there are those who claim that truth is not only knowable, but is in fact, known and only the stubborn recalcitrance of the uninitiated prevents it from being generally accepted. This point of view claims not only that morality exists as a discoverable truth, an absolute not fashioned by men but unchanging and immutable, but also that truth has in fact been discovered. Rights and wrongs exist quite apart from the stage on which their application is played out. Situations may differ but, at most, such differences force us to reinterpret old and forever valid principles in a new light. Those who believe themselves to know the truth, furthermore, oftentimes feel compelled not only to persuade others to their point of view but feel morally justified in using considerable force to do so.

On the other hand, some of us would deny the existence of immutable truth or, what is not quite the same thing, deny at least that it is knowable in the human condition. Those who flatly deny the existence of unalterable truth find themselves in much the same pickle as do those who flatly assert it: Both lack a standard of truth to which their affirmations can be appealed. Those who concede the possibility that truth exists but not the possibility that man in the human condition can be privy to it, have modified the position without greatly improving it. Their affirmation that man in the human condition can never know absolute truth seems more reasonable but is, once again, not verifiable. Who can know with certainty that tomorrow someone will not discover a way of "getting at" absolute truth and, in addition, be able to provide a simple and brilliant proof which other mortals to date have missed? Only an absolutist could deny such a possibility!

That leaves us with a more pragmatic answer: Holding that, in the human condition, truth is not—or at least is not currently—accessible to us leaves more options open and does not fly in the face of the undeniable fact that, unlikely as it seems, our knowing absolute truth may be just around the corner. Outside the religious sphere, no one has ever convinced most thinking people that they are the possessors of absolute truth. Truth, whenever accepted at least for daily use, is invariably hedged.

If we accept the fact that absolute truth (at least so far) is unknown to us and accept as an axiom that it may well be unknowable, we are left with a truth which for everyday use is fashioned rather than discovered. What is and what is not true or what is and what is not morally acceptable, therefore, varies with the culture in which we live. This claim (the claim on which, as we shall see, cultural relativism relies) rests on the assertion that there are many ways of looking at truths and that such truths are fashioned by people. Depending on our vantage point, there are many visions of reality,[1] a fact which the defenders of this doctrine hold to be valid in dealing with the concrete, scientific reality of chemistry and physics.[2] Such a claim, it would seem, is even more forceful when dealing with morals. As Engelhardt puts it so very well: "Our construals of reality exist within the embrace of cultural expectations."[3] And our "construals of reality" include our vision of the moral life. Furthermore, not only do our "visions of reality occur within the embrace of cultural expectations," the limits of what we as humans can and what we cannot culturally (or otherwise) expect are biologically framed by the totality of our bodies and their capacities as well as (and inseparable from the rest of the body of which it is a part) by our minds.

All human judgments and decisions, then, are inevitably grounded in prior assumptions which we accept and do not question for now. There is a story about William James which illustrates the point. James was giving a lecture dealing with the universe at a Chattauqua: one of those events so popular at the turn of the century, which has, regrettably, been replaced by talk shows. At the end of his well-received lecture, a little old lady came up to him and said: "I enjoyed your talk, Mr. James, but you know you are making an error: The universe rests on the back of a tortoise!" James, for the sake of argument, agreed but asked what, then, the tortoise rested upon? "Why, Mr. James, it rests upon another tortoise!" "Very well,"James said, "I can accept that. But tell me, what in turn does that other tortoise rest upon?" "It's no use, Mr. James, it's tortoises all the way down." And so it goes: Every assumption rests on the back of another assumption and if we are to examine all before proceeding with our everyday judgments and decisions we would get hopelessly mired in mud. The quest is necessarily endless.

Ethical theories, like all other human activities, inevitably rest on prior assumptions. Indeed, one cannot reason without a framework of reasoning, and similarly, one cannot reason about reasoning without such a prior framework. The question, it seems, is not the necessary acceptance of an assumption, for that is inevitable, but the depth and universality of the assumption taken. One needs steer between Scylla and Charybdis: on one side too-easy acceptance of a superficial assumption, on the other an endless and almost neurotic quest for ever more basic assumptions. Shattering on the first cliff leads one to an analysis of problems which is inevitably unpersuasive to those not sharing the same prior assumptions. Crashing on the other condemns one to eternal philosophical backpedaling, inactivity, and to leaving the original problem, whose immediate resolution may be critically needed, entirely unresolved.

That some framework of reasoning is necessary was recognized by Kant when he claimed that, thanks to the "common structure of our mind," thought processes inevitably divided the sensible world into categories which we then use to deal with it.[4] Rationality requires ways of dealing with the world and reasoning without categories is evidently not possible. The reason why there is no disagreement among persons about some logical propositions is that the common structure of our mind compels us to see certain things in certain ways and to reason along certain lines made inevitable by the very way in which our minds are structured. Even if, later on, we may discover that our universally agreed-upon proposition was wrong, we make this discovery using the same tools. We merely discover that some crucial fact was missing, some critical point not considered. The same basic method of reasoning and the same biological substrate for reasoning (the common structure of our mind) has been used to discover our error.

I do not claim that our common biology and the common structure of our minds constitutes a way of discovering absolute truth. What such a common biology and such a common structure imply is that we inevitably will approach problems, see truth, and derive our judgments within such a bodily framework. We are condemned (or blessed) to know the sensible world and to reason from the data presented to us and organized by us in certain and not in other ways. That does not reveal truth to us, but it presents us with a working model to be used, adapted, and learned from.

The belief that there are no absolutes (or that, at the very least, they are inaccessible to us in the human condition) can lead to a moral nihilism in which no firm judgments can be made and no decisions or actions can be undertaken. Such a moral nihilism claims that truths are fashioned by people and however a person may choose to fashion his truths serves no better than does any other way of constructing truths. The fashioning of truths, in that point of view, lacks its own frame of reference. It does not necessarily follow from this, however, that since our "construals of reality" occur purely within the "embrace of cultural expectations," all visions of reality are necessarily of equal worth, or that there are no generally useful standards that we can employ in judging either what we conceive to be physical or ethical reality. One can, for example, claim that some visions of reality are clearly and demonstrably wrong, and support such a claim by empirical observation or by showing that certain visions of reality simply do not work. That is the stronger claim. In rejoinder, it can be said that empirical observations and "what works" are themselves part of the framework and that, therefore, such a claim lacks validity.

On the other hand, one can make the somewhat weaker claim that certain visions, in the context of a given society and historical epoch, seem less valid than others because they confound careful observation or because they simply fail to work when applied to real situations occurring in real current societies.[5] This leaves room for a form of modified cultural relativism. Such a move does not deny that our "visions of reality occur within the embrace of cultural expectations." But while such a move affirms that there are many realities of similar worth, it also suggests that within the context of such cultural expectations some realities have little, and others much, validity. Some realities work (have explanatory power translatable into action and are, therefore, usable) in the context of our experience and community, while some do not, and some work better than do others. Such a view neither throws up its hands and grants automatic equal worth nor rigidly enforces one view: It looks upon the problem as one of learning and growth in which realities (both empirical and ethical) are neither rigidly fixed nor entirely subject to ad hoc interpretation.

Ethical certitude, no more than certitude about anything else, is not possible in the human condition. The "ut in pluribus," the generally and for the most part true of which St. Thomas Aquinas speaks, is the best we can hope for in science as well as in ethics. Since, however, we must inevitably act (nonaction being as much action as action itself), we must be prepared to act on less than complete certitude. Truth cannot, in a Cartesian sense, be expected to be apodictic; rather truth (whether it is scientific or moral truth) is to be worked with, shaped and developed as we experience, learn, and grow.

That moral truths, like other truths, are not rigidly fixed but are subject to social structuring and ongoing growth and learning is for many an uncomfortable thought. Many would much prefer to have predetermined principles and cookie-cutting rules according to which they can tailor their lives and to which they can quite thoughtlessly adapt their behavior. Those who accept rigid rules and predetermined principles as normative are saddled with at least two troubling problems. (1) When one tries to fit rules and principles to a context from and for which they were not created (say, try to thoughtlessly jam the Kantian injunction of truth telling on all clinical encounters) the results are often unfortunate and the fit is obviously poor. (2) When one tries to justify the rules themselves, one often finds that the rules themselves are the assumptions or that the assumptions on which they rest are not supported either by other defensible ones or even by common sense. Furthermore, following predetermined normative principles can deny the very enterprise in which we allegedly are engaged: the exercise of moral choice. If moral choice is to emanate from a moral agent instead of from a machine, it must be the result of the agent's free and thoughtful choosing not a predetermined response made on purely legalistic and unthinking grounds. The merit of ethical choosing resides not so much in the specific choice made as it does in the agony of decision making. The essence of the agony is the sifting and sorting which moral agents willingly undertake to reach a specific choice. Flipping a coin because we do not want to be bothered, or applying a predetermined absolute principle for the same reason, abrogates our first duty as moral agents: making deliberate, carefully thought out, intelligently conceived, and compassionate choices. And when we make such choices we use, consciously or otherwise, a framework for decision making.

In making ethical judgments, we usually refer these judgments either to consequences or use principles determined by other means. Consequentialist ethics judges actions or rules to be good or bad according to the consequences brought about. A rule or action which serves to bring about the greatest amount of good for the greatest number of people is the right rule or action. Those, on the other hand, who would deny that rules or actions can be judged in this way will advance the claim that outcomes are often beyond our ability to foretell and that, therefore, one cannot use consequences to judge either rules or actions. Intention, not outcome, is what matters. The two opposing points of view, of course, are exemplified by utilitarianism on the one and deontology on the other hand. Mill and Kant are the two most notorious representatives of these schools.[6,7]

For utilitarians, be they act or rule utilitarians, the eventual bringing about of the greatest good for the greatest number is the issue. Consequences are what matter. This ethic makes a very commonsense appeal to us. Surely, we are interested in how we live and, therefore, in the consequences of our actions and our neighbor's actions. Intentions are well and good, but the road to hell is, as has so often been said, paved with good intentions.

Of course, there is a problem with that stance. Consequences are not only unpredictable, what is and what is not the greatest good for the greatest number is, for several reasons, problematic. How does one determine what is and what is not good? It is hardly the case that people agree on even very fundamental goods. Unless the nature of the good is defined, striving for the greatest good is surely difficult. (Working out the nature of the good by political means, as Aristotle suggests, rather than determining it for all times is one of the most crucial functions of ethical inquiry.) How is the greatest number to be determined? By a simple addition in which all count equally no matter what their status, capacity, or prior history? How are clashes of values to be resolved? Say, a community has funds to provide either an educational program or slap-stick comedy: Is serving the greatest good to be construed as doing what gives satisfaction to the larger number? And is such satisfaction reckoned on a short- or long-term basis? Such questions aside, can bringing about a great good by evil means be considered an unalloyed good? For example, a healthy person without social attachments (and, therefore, a person whose death would not greatly matter to anyone) is secretly killed in order to harvest her organs and therefore save several lives. Is this truly a good thing to do? If not, why not? Clearly these two fundamental problems (the unpredictability of consequences and the nature of what we consider as good) cannot be brushed away.

Deontologists deny the validity of the utilitarian presumptions. Consequences are not what matters. Only intentions matter. Moral laws are established not because the greatest number would benefit but because they are commanded by the reason common to all sentient beings and because, therefore, they could be willed to be universal law. Sentient beings are moral agents: able to self-legislate their own moral law. That such a law must universalize (that it could be "willed to be a law of nature" or, in other words, that in a particular instance and under particular circumstances the action I choose must with equal force and under the same circumstances be permissible for others) is the essential part of the doctrine. An action done because it conforms to such a law (not merely because one is inclined to do it without regard for the law) is praiseworthy; one which violates such a law, blameworthy. Because humans have the capacity to self-legislate moral law, they are worthy of respect and must never be used "merely as a means but always also as an end in themselves."[4] Following such a law may have unintended consequences but these are hardly the agent's fault and, therefore, do not make him blameworthy.

There are a host of difficulties here also. First of all, just as in utilitarianism, the definition of the good is at best vague. The good is seen as the product of self-legislation and universalization, perhaps a product of the common biological structure of our minds. Beyond this, and the converse of one of the problems with utilitarianism, an action taken with the best of intentions but that brings about terrible consequences cannot ordinarily be seen as an unalloyed good. Killing someone inadvertently and with the best intentions cannot, ultimately, be a good thing. By being well intentioned (that is, by following a universalizable act of self-legislation) it may have been the right action but it was hardly an unreservedly fine thing to do. (W. D. Ross[8] differentiates between "rightness," a property belonging to acts instead of motives and "goodness" a property belonging to the motive of the act in question: Here I am using these words in a somewhat different sense.) Further and perhaps even more problematic is the fact that framing what we want to do in such a way that it becomes permissible and that it would universalize is not altogether difficult. As Kant says: The only thing good in itself and without reservation is the good will; but judging what is and what is not a good will (knowing whether another really self-legislates in a moral way and is intent on following such a law) is quite another matter.

Others would have morality purely situational,[9,10] merely dependent upon the specifics of the situation at hand. With such an approach, however, we are apt to lack a reference point. Making each solution dependent upon maximizing the good, or upon bringing about the greatest amount of love, has been suggested as the proper guide. But such solutions leave the "good" and "love" undefined. The danger of substituting our own idiosyncratic vision of the good, or applying our own or our particular moral enclave's definition of love, is then very great. It is precisely this danger of idiosyncratic vision which is the reason for the insistence upon universalizability. Universalizability, it seems, can be a hedge against the extremes of cultural relativism. The point of view which would look at each situation as entirely unique and judgable only on its own terms is the view originally advanced by Fletcher and called "situationalism." Even when situationalism takes place in a framework of general rules, "rules of thumb" as Fletcher would have it, the rules which in turn must determine these rules of thumb must necessarily conform to some prior insight of the good or of love. Such a prior insight, in turn, either is the product of rigidly conceived truth or will be seen to vary from society to society in its definition.

The formation of character so that the agent will, by habit, make good moral choices, or "virtue ethics" as it has been called, is a most appealing ethical framework. To become skilled in moral discernment and to make, therefore, habitually proper ethical choices is, after all, the legitimate goal of the ethical life.[11] Such a skill in making moral choices comes from a careful analysis of specific cases and rules from a consideration of groupings of similar cases which then provide guidelines.[12] This ethic of casuistry has much to recommend it in daily life and especially in a clinical setting. Is not the person whose ethical behavior we look up to a person who can be relied upon to make ethically good choices? The problem, with this as well as with situational ethics, is that a judgment of what is and what is not a good choice depends upon its own frame of reference. No amount of skill in making choices can determine whether the choices made were or were not good. Depending on a specific external standard of what is and what is not a good choice, one could very well develop skill in making incredibly bad moral choices habitually. Only a prior framework of what constitutes a good choice can establish a base on which to build. I hope to show that such a framework can be established by considerations of suffering and worked out by and in a community.

Cultural relativists will advance the claim that what is and what is not good is purely variable from society to society and is not fixed over time and space. This notion is grounded (1) in the observation by anthropologists that mores and notions of right and wrong differ, often dramatically, from culture to culture, (2) on the assumption that absolute truth either does not exist or is inaccessible to us in the human condition and (3) on the conclusion that all truths (including all moral points of view) enjoy equal validity. In other words, anything goes! Cultural relativism, however, also seems to have a prior framework. It is a framework in which certain traits seem fundamental to all groups studied. All of these groups have communities, kinship groups, and all individuals within these groups have a common capacity to suffer and to try their best to evade it. Even if we grant the vast differences in the mores of one from that of another group, certain common ideas and ways of behaving exist. Such common ideas and ways of behaving are the result of the common framework which the body and its limitations imposes. Although details of expression vary biosocial needs are transcultural.

Consider the Babylonian peasant reared in a small community, a community whose integrity is believed to be safeguarded by the annual sacrifice of a selected firstborn to Moloch. Should such a peasant, when his firstborn is selected for sacrifice, be held blameworthy for sacrificing his child? Or, on the contrary, could a refusal to yield his son be held to be an immoral act endangering the whole village for the sake of his own selfish interests? By what standards are we to judge? By our own standards, by those of his society, or by an absolute to whose knowledge we pretend?

But, hold on! Judging the peasant's blameworthiness is not quite the same thing as judging the act to be right or wrong. The peasant may, in his special context, not be to blame: His intentions were good, he acted according to his own conscience and, from his point of view, he helped ensure the safety of the entire community. And yet, the act of infant sacrifice may, on the whole, still be considered wrong. If so, this judgment must accord to some universal principle that all could subscribe to. In judging our Babylonian peasant as blame- or praiseworthy, we cannot apply today's standard to an ancient situation. In judging the act (apart from the actor), we cannot, on the other hand, apply ancient mores to today's judgments. What is our peasant to do? Even if the good were knowable, whose good is to be maximized and how is love to be expressed? Is it not the case that he, like all of us, is forced to do good and to express love purely according to his own vision (formed within his peculiar "cultural embrace")? And, in that case, is not morality purely a matter of situation and personal vision?

Appealing as such act-utilitarianism or agapism is, it breaks down when one considers that what is right is not necessarily merely determined by the good that is brought about.[13] Other factors matter: Bringing about what is seen as a good circumstance by reprehensible means or performing an accidentally good deed (in terms of its outcome) with evil intentions cannot be considered an untarnished good. Saving a life by breaking a promise may make the act of saving a life a good act but it does not, therefore, make the breaking of a promise a good thing. Saving a life is good both because what is brought about is, except under unusual circumstances, held to be logically good (under usual circumstances maintaining a life desired by its subject universalizes) and because it conforms to a socially accepted vision of what "good" is. Promise-breaking, on the other hand, cannot be logically universalized (speech that does not presuppose truth-telling is pointless) and is contrary to a socially accepted vision of the good. An agent, furthermore, may intend to do harm, but inadvertantly bring about good; the act is good in its consequences but bad in its intention. With our peasant and viewed from our vantage point, that act was bad in as far as the child is concerned and irrelevant for the village (no harm would have, in fact, resulted from its omission), but the intentions were good.

It may be that judgments about given situations are judgments which often paint with too broad a brush when they call the act good or bad. (Ross, as we have seen, differentiates between motives which are good or bad and acts which are right or wrong. However, a prior vision of good/bad or right/wrong, which Ross essentially finds in intuitionism must be assumed[8]). Discriminating between the consequences of an act (and judging that consequence good or bad) and separately dealing with the intention (and judging it separately as good or bad) allows finer analysis. In failing to separate the intention of the actor from the outcome of an act, holding either that an act is good or bad because of the intention of the actor or, on the other hand, that it is good or bad regardless of intention, we muddy the water.[14,15] While an act may be so enmeshed in its intention that we cannot effectively separate the two, we can still distinguish one from the other in our minds.

Judgments about acts and about actors cannot be reduced merely to intention or consequence, any more than intentions or consequences can simply be ignored. The claim that either a utilitarian or a deontological system must be employed and that utilitarianism and deontology are quite incompatible has usually been advanced. I shall claim, to the contrary, that utilitarianism and deontology necessarily presuppose each other. When Kant speaks of intention, it is the intention *to bring about a consequence*: one cannot it seems, have an intention without this. To intend something, is to wish to bring about a consequence.

Even when we look at an act and say that it is the right thing to do despite the consequences the act may have, the connection between intention and consequence holds true. Instead of willing the material consequence of such an act we may accept a bad material consequence in order to perform what we consider to be a right act. And, ultimately, we have judged it to be right because of the consequences such acts commonly entail. On the other hand, when utilitarians or agapists set out to maximize the good (or to bring about a situation most conforming to a loving outcome), their vision of what it is to do good, or to be loving, is unavoidably rooted in a prior vision of the good. This prior vision of the good conforms to a logically universalizable principle (the particular vision of love or good entailed must be universalizable) as well as to a preexisting social vision (the particular notions of love and good current in a particular society). The nature of such a universalizable principle in turn must conform to the limits imposed by human biology.[14,15]

If morality is not to be purely situational, entirely dependent upon the cultural context and adapting itself to an ill-defined good, or be predicated on ill-defined love, and if morality cannot be conceived as absolute rules unbendingly binding under all situations, how can one determine some transcendental basis on which one can then begin to build? I believe that such a basis can be rationally carved out and cautiously employed as a ground for further exploration. The ground of such an ethic is a biological one, enunciated, applied, and modified in the embrace of community. It is predicated on our common biology and consequently our common "structure of the mind" which enables all sentient creatures (be they parakeets, chimpanzees, or humans) to appreciate benefit and harm. If, as we claim, ethics is of necessity other-directed, then the capacity, now or in the future, to be capable of perceiving benefit or harm becomes central to it. Such a perception of benefit and harm is not purely a biological one: It is not purely benefit and harm in terms of pain or pleasure as perceived by our body. Rather, benefit and harm is conditioned by and experienced in community. Humans, as well as animals, share the capacity to suffer even when, as they must, they define suffering individually. The community to which all belong, both the narrower community which shapes our personal perception and experience and the community of our common biology which determines our shared capacities, forms the terrain on which our experiences are played out and our attitudes are developed. An ethic based on the capacity to suffer gives entities moral worth because of that capacity and obliges us to refrain from capriciously causing such entities to suffer. Entities who share in the capacity to suffer have a knowing interest in not suffering and, in general, are capable of having an interest in spinning out their life and its experiences.

The capacity to suffer, the ability to perceive benefit or, at least, harm is central to any of our questions of morality. Since rocks cannot suffer, it is difficult to speak of acting in a morally blameworthy fashion towards a rock. One cannot, in that sense, harm a rock in itself. The moral question comes up only when damaging the rock would cause suffering to another. And it is the capacity to suffer, rather than the capacity to experience pleasure, that is central to my thesis. This is the case because the capacity to suffer is a biologically more fundamental one: A person may (when severely senile, for example) entirely lose the capacity to experience joy but retain the capacity to suffer. The old woman lying in a fetal position in a nursing home, generally unaware of her environment but evidently made uncomfortable when tied down, derives only a passive sort of pleasure by not being made to suffer. Experiencing pleasure is, as it were, a higher function: one requiring a further integrative step of existence. We cannot bring pleasure to such beings, but, at the very least, we ought not to make them capriciously suffer. It is possible to make persons capable of experiencing pleasure suffer; but it is not always possible to make those capable of suffering experience pleasure. Not capriciously making entities capable of suffering suffer, and beyond this to do what is possible to ameliorate suffering, is a deeper grounding than bringing pleasure. Such a stance underpins some of the recent anti-cruelty policies suggested in medical ethics.[16]

Giving moral standing to entities capable of suffering and assigning a primary prima facie obligation to an injunction against causing such suffering could, it will be said, open the door to allowing painless killing. After all, when my life is suddenly and painlessly extinguished in the midst of writing this book, no suffering can occur. It is here that the injunction against causing suffering to entities with a current or future capacity to suffer becomes important. Extinguishing my life plans, abrogating my possibilities and terminating my capacity to suffer (or enjoy) can be seen as a most grievous interference. Wantonly and without the entity's expressed desire terminating the life of an entity equipped with a functioning or potentially functioning neocortex and limbic system (and thus of an entity capable of present or future suffering) is not an act to be taken lightly.

The prima facie injunction against making entities suffer who are capable of it is, it seems, a necessary condition of acting morally. It is, however, an insufficient one. Not causing another to suffer is more fundamental than either ameliorating suffering or trying to give pleasure. Ameliorating suffering or attempting to give pleasure to entities capable of experiencing pleasure is, as we shall later argue, a more optional moral obligation. There are analogies to this both as pertains to personal ethics (autonomy versus beneficence) and when it comes to communal issues.

Obligations of autonomy and beneficence are linked: To be truly beneficent is to have a healthy respect for autonomous choice. It is not possible to be beneficent and disregard such an obligation.[17] However, the converse does not hold: Respect for autonomy entails no obligation of beneficence. To attempt to ameliorate suffering wherever possible or, a step beyond, to give pleasure whenever possible, one must first refrain from causing suffering. A life in which no suffering but also no pleasure occurs is empty, just as is an ethic devoted to autonomy but bereft of beneficence. But ameliorating suffering or bringing about pleasure is a lesser obligation than is refraining from causing suffering since not causing suffering is always possible even if it may not always be worthwhile (as a prima facie obligation the injunction not to cause suffering may, for weighty reasons, be overruled). On the other hand, callously making another suffer but claiming to be concerned about their pleasure makes as much sense as violating autonomy in the pursuit of beneficence.

The relationship between the issues of social justice and private liberty likewise bears a similarity to suffering and pleasure. One may take Stalinist communism, in which social justice without individual liberty existed, as one example and contrast it with a capitalist system, in which individual rights are supposedly guaranteed but communitarian concerns and social justice are given little standing. Without social justice, giving autonomy and freedom to all members of a community becomes a mockery for those deprived of the necessary basis of existence. Having the freedom to assemble or to speak freely is not comforting for those freezing or starving to death. On the other hand, providing the necessities of life but denying personal liberties makes of life a thing not very well worth living. Having a warm shelter and sufficient food without having the opportunity for pursuing one's own vision of the good and without the personal opportunity to flourish, cannot provide satisfaction. This book is largely devoted to arguing for social justice as well as for personal liberties as mutually reinforcing rather than as separate or separable entities. Such an argument is based on the shared capacity for suffering, on a prima facie obligation against causing others suffering, and a derivative obligation to ameliorate such suffering where possible.

A prima facie obligation not to make entities capable of suffering suffer capriciously would seem to need little defense. The burden of proof, one might argue, is on those who look upon the infliction of capricious suffering with moral indifference. However, a defense for such a proposition is easily seen in the fact that, because of its inherent logic, such a proposition universalizes: We cannot callously inflict suffering under a given set of circumstances upon another entity capable of suffering without allowing them to do the same to us. Such an argument, of course, assumes the rightness of the universalizability principle. It is an assumption in turn based on the common biological structure of our mind that compels us to see logic in certain but not in other ways. Those who believe themselves not to be bound by this stricture are, by that virtue, labeled psychopathic. If the good, in Kantian terms is seen as the product of self-legislation and universalization underpinned by the common structure of our mind, such a good is biologically determined. The obligation to ameliorate suffering where possible is an obligation not so much grounded in logic (one can, as Kant maintains, logically will a world without imperfect duties such as beneficence[7]) as in common experience: All of us being in need of compassion and help at some time of our lives could not truly will a world in which compassion and beneficence played no role. Such a wish, as Kant has pointed out, would "force the will to conflict with itself."[7]

Humans, like perhaps to a lesser extent other sentient beings, are social beings with the capacity to reflect on themselves, on their existence, and on their universe. This capacity implies the ability to reflect on others as well as on the environment. Sentient beings must do this if they are to deal on a more than reflex level with their environment and with others. All humans (at least all humans we consider nonpsychopathic and within our perception of what is normal), when confronted with the misery of another truly, feel a sense of unease, a sense that there is something very wrong and that they too are suffering. This sense of "suffering or experiencing with"[18] (the German *Mitleiden*, or the Dutch *Medeleiden*, is exactly translatable as "suffering with") which implies the ability to put oneself in the place of another is a biologically normal response of humans and perhaps of other organisms; it is part of what it means to "reflect on others and on their environment." When we can "put ourselves in the place of another" we can begin to understand how and why that other acts and can begin to relate with her or him. This sense of compassion is a biological trait and one closely connected with what Rousseau calls a "natural sense of pity."[19]

Compassion has a very direct bearing on the sort of ethic developed here. Compassion, the feeling in us inspired by the perceived or actual suffering of others, is what makes an ethic based on suffering operative. Without compassion the suffering of others leaves us cold and, at best, we develop an icy and austere ethic inspired only by a duty of logic. Such an ethic counsels obedience because to do otherwise would be irrational. Obedience to the most rational precept for solving a problem is, however, only possible after the existence of the problem has entered our consciousness as a problem. Without compassion, the moral problem can easily escape us: The suffering of others and the moral problems engendered by such suffering may not even enter our moral consciousness. Rousseau remarked that all humans, even in the "primitive state of nature" prior to the emergence of a social contract (and according to him, therefore, prior to the development of a socially conditioned moral sense), were endowed with a "natural sense of pity."[20] It is this "natural sense of pity," this inability to view the suffering of other fellow creatures with equanimity which underpins, initiates, and is perhaps equivalent to the sense of compassion. It, therefore, helps to make any ethic and any ethical sensitivity operative. If ethics, as we claim, is necessarily other-directed, no ethical action is likely to come about without sensitivity to the existence of the problem and without compassion for it. The coldest individuals, bent merely on doing their logical duty will need some sense of pity, some sense of compassion, to become truly aware of the problem and to stir awareness into action.

At best, an ethic finding its roots in an entity's capacity for suffering and not firmly anchored in a well-developed sense of compassion will be an ethic which will be concerned merely with refraining from causing others to suffer. In Kantian terms, it will be an ethic concerned purely with the "perfect" duties of refraining from doing something and heedless of the "imperfect" duties of ameliorating.[7] Not making others suffer may be accepted and recognized as an obligation even when actively doing something about the suffering of others is not. Once the existence of the capacity to suffer is recognized in others (which already implies the capacity to reflect on others and on their feelings and, therefore, necessarily entails some compassion) and once those things causing another to suffer are acknowledged, logical duty will counsel one not to cause such suffering. A sense of pity and a well-developed sense of compassion, however, goes beyond this: It counsels us to accept the obligation to ameliorate as well as not to cause suffering. Such a counsel is based, first of all, less in logic than in a well-developed sense of compassion and in the realization that all of us at one time or another are in direct and often dire need of each other's help. Such a realization comes to us as we reflect on others and on our environment. (As I will show later, duties of refraining from harm to one another without concommittant duties of benefitting each other are grounded in a Hobbesian vision of community forged in mutual terror.) Furthermore, such a counsel can be seen as an expression of a Rawlsian veil of ignorance: (a veil behind which a prudent person not knowing what his/her particular fate might be must make choices). Behind such a veil and not knowing what life holds for us, the prudent chooser would choose to maximize compassion.[21]

Using the capacity to suffer as a grounding for developing a moral structure can in many ways unite consequential and nonconsequential points of view. The capacity to suffer is a universal capacity one which, by definition, unites all sentient creatures. One cannot be sentient and lack it. Not bringing capricious suffering to those endowed with that capacity has logical force by virtue of its being a notion which all sentient beings can readily understand, acquiesce to, and embrace. On the other hand, such an ethic is outcome-directed: It seeks to minimize suffering and, in formulating hierarchies, will pay some but not total attention to what may or may not be best for most. Moreover, the effort to ameliorate suffering where possible seeks to bring about not only a universal good but a good for the greatest number of members. I am not trying to make of the prevention of suffering the "summum bonum." I am merely justifying and appealing such a definition of a good (one good among many outcome-directed goods) by relating it to the common experience of all sentient beings.

If one accepts that the capacity to suffer endows an entity with prima facie rights against being made to suffer and with legitimate expectations that others in the community will, where possible, ameliorate suffering, one can accept suffering as a possible ground for obligation. Such a concept provides more than merely an empty and abstract form. It allows a concrete content whose usefulness is broad enough to readily accommodate to the form without distorting it. The range of the concept and the range of the content are identical. Epistemologically, it bridges the traditional gap between form and content. In such an ethic the prohibition against causing suffering to others is not an absolute condition, but causing suffering to others capable of suffering needs to be justified. The ability to suffer is what separates rocks, who cannot suffer, from puppies or college students, who can.[20]

Not causing other entities to suffer, then, cannot be a moral absolute. After all, we frequently and in our daily lives have little choice but to cause others to suffer. I suggest that the fundamental prohibition against causing suffering to other entities capable of it is a prima facie duty. Entities that have the capacity now or in the future to suffer have a prima facie right not to be made to suffer and share the legitimate expectation that, where possible, all will be done to alleviate suffering. This is a fundamental right and one which can be overturned only with good reason. Prima facie rights and prima facie duties are such because they are enjoyed (or must be performed) unless compelling reasons to the contrary can be shown.

Prima facie conditions require moral discernment. They require a careful dissecting out of hierarchies of values so that, ultimately, each can be allowed to override those below it. When such a process is done in a biological framework a common vision of logic, and therefore, a common vision of rationality is imposed. But in addition, it is a process which occurs in the context of particular communities and social conditions. Thus our cultural expectations, of which Engelhardt speaks so eloquently, are expectations conditioned and limited by our biology and formed by and in our communities. When I come to discuss social contract, communities and the obligations which emanate from such views, the "sense of pity" and compassion will once again form the tacit background of such an argument. Without such a sense, social contract and community are empty and, except perhaps in a strictly Hobbesian way, not even possible. Compassion, arising from what Rousseau saw as a "primitive sense of pity" and perhaps in a sense equivalent to it, is what gives individual as well as social ethics body and substance. Without it, ethics easily becomes mere legalism.

If one is to accept an ethic based on the capacity to suffer, one needs at the very least to suggest hierarchies of values. Inevitably, showing hierarchies of values requires the articulation of such values in the embrace of our particular vision of community. To develop a notion of our mutual obligations one needs to suggest ways of delineating hierarchies and one must develop a vision of community. It is this endeavor to which the rest of the book is devoted.

## References

1. Fleck L: *Genesis and Development of a Scientific Fact.* T. J. Trenn and R. K. Merton eds., F. Bradley and T. J. Trenn, trans. Chicago: University of Chicago Press, 1979.

2. Kuhn T: *The Structure of Scientific Revolutions.* Chicago: University of Chicago Press, 1970.

3. Engelhardt HT: *Foundations of Bioethics.* New York: Oxford University Press, 1986.

4. Kant I: *Critique of Pure Reason.* N. K. Smith, trans. New York: St. Martin's Press, 1965.

5. Loewy EH: Communities, Self-Causation and the Natural Lottery. *Soc Sci & Med* 26:1133-39, 1988.

6. Mill JS: *Utilitarianism*. Indianapolis: Bobbs-Merrill, 1979.

7. Kant I: *Foundations of Metaphysics of Morals*. C. W. Beck, trans. Indianapolis: Bobbs-Merrill, 1980.

8. Ross WD: *The Foundations of Ethics*. Oxford: Clarendon Press, 1939.

9. Fletcher J: *Situation Ethics*. Philadelphia: Westminster Press, 1966.

10. Fletcher J: Situation Ethics Revisited. *Religious Humanism* 16:9-13, 1982.

11. MacIntyre A: *After Virtue*. Notre Dame, IN: University of Notre Dame Press, 1984.

12. Jonsen AR, Toulmin S: *The Abuses of Casuistry*. Berkeley: University of California Press, 1988.

13. Frankena WK: *Ethics*. Englewood Cliffs, NJ: Prentice Hall, 1973.

14. Loewy EH: Suffering, Moral Worth and Medical Ethics: A New Beginning. *Bridges* 1(3/4):103-17, 1989.

15. Loewy EH: The Role of Suffering and Community in Clinical Ethics. *J Clin Ethics* 1(2), 1990, (in publication).

16. Braithwaite S, Thomasma DC: New Guidelines on Forgoing Life-Sustaining Treatment in Incompetent Patients: An Anti-Cruelty Policy. *Ann Int Med* 104:711-15, 1986.

17. Pellegrino ED, Thomasma DC: *For the Patient's Good: The Restoration of Beneficence to Health Care*. New York: Oxford University Press, 1988.

18. Reich WT: Speaking of Suffering: A Moral Account of Compassion. *Soundings* 72(1):83-108, 1989.

19. Rousseau JJ: *Du Contrat Social*. R. Grimsley, ed. Oxford: Oxford University Press, 1972.

20. Loewy EH: Obligations, Communities and Suffering: Problems of Community Seen in a New Light. *Bridges* 2(1):1-16, 1990.

21. Rawls J: *A Theory of Justice*. Cambridge: Harvard University Press, 1971.

# Chapter Three

# Moral Worth: Kinds and Hierarchies

In this chapter, I will use the capacity to suffer as a moral basis to examine ways of establishing categories and hierarchies of moral worth. In the previous chapter, I have argued that entities who now or in the future have the capacity to suffer are entities endowed with moral worth. Such entities sharing the capacity now or in the future to suffer are the entities which form the framework of our ethical considerations and obligations. If we accept the capacity to suffer as a ground for moral concern, we must, whenever possible, refrain from hurting another who can appreciate such hurt. This, in the point of view presented here, is the necessary but insufficient condition of acting in a moral fashion. It is insufficient because merely refraining from hurting another does not exhaust moral obligation: Beyond this an obligation exists to ameliorate suffering and, perhaps in a much weaker way to, where possible, give pleasure.

While the injunction against hurting another seems clear enough, it is an injunction which is neither capable of being adhered to perfectly nor one which, morally speaking, gets us very far. There are times when hurting another is inevitable, other times when hurting another seems preferable to some other action. Some actions, furthermore, do not directly hurt another and still are intuitively felt to be reprehensible. Polluting the environment, burning books, damaging cars, or desecrating prayer shawls would serve as examples. And yet the environment, as well as books, cars, and prayer shawls, cannot, except in an allegorical sense, be said to suffer. Furthermore, there are times when we may feel entitled to make another suffer so as to avoid polluting the environment or damaging books, cars, or prayer shawls. It seems that our grounding has not gotten us very far.

In this chapter, I will sketch out a division of moral worth into primary, secondary and (a subset of secondary) symbolic areas without suggesting that these are necessarily or inevitably in hierarchical order. I will then try to suggest some ways of approaching the necessary task of carving out reasonable hierarchies both within these separate categories and among them so that everyday judgments can be made. I shall categorize entities with an inherent capacity to suffer as being of primary worth and will categorize objects who lack this capacity but which are important from an ethical standpoint as being objects of secondary worth. This second group I will also divide into subclassifications of material and symbolic worth. After suggesting these categories, I will then map out some of the possible ways in which hierarchies of worth within these categories can be established, and I will address the equally difficult problem of the value relationship among these classifications. I will try to show that such a schema has theoretical merit as well as having flexibility and, therefore, adaptability for examining many practical ethical problems.

Entities considered to be of primary worth are those entities which now or in the future may be aware of their suffering. This includes college students, small children, temporarily unconscious or anaesthetized patients as well as embryos, dogs, cows, and parakeets, all of whom have (or, in the case of embryos, possess a potential for having—a matter which we will take up later) a neocortex and a limbic system. The presence (or potential presence) of the neocortex and of the limbic system constitutes the necessary precondition for the capacity to suffer. The category of entities of primary worth does not include such things as bacteria or other forms of life bereft of a neocortex or of a limbic system and it does not include the environment or nonliving objects. Entities which have a neocortex as well as a limbic system (entities which, in other words, have the actual or potential physical substrate for suffering) have an important prima facie claim against being made to suffer; when suffering must be produced there is a prima facie obligation to justify it and a prima facie assumption that to cause suffering is blameworthy. Acts or rules which would cause suffering are morally allowable only under circumstances when justification can be shown to be valid. Grounds for making such justification, then, need to be carved out.

Entities of secondary worth are those valued by others who themselves are of primary worth. Damaging an entity of secondary worth would cause suffering not in the entity being damaged but in the entity doing the valuing. Damaging a car is wrong if the car is valued by another. Obviously, the amount of secondary worth depends on such valuing and varies with time and place. The same object may gain or lose worth.

Secondary value, furthermore, may be negative and be expressed in disvalue. I may, for example, greatly fear the rock perched on a hill over my house, and breaking the rock (damaging it) would allow me to breathe a sigh of relief. Such an object, rather than being valued (and therefore enjoying a prima facie protection against being harmed) is disvalued and harming it would benefit one of primary worth. In an ethic based on the shared capacity for suffering, not harming another (or not harming something another values) is a direct obligation derived from the logical underpinnings of the ethic. Destroying an object that is disvalued (removing a threat or preventing the suffering of another, for example) has a somewhat different standing: it is an obligation akin to Kant's imperfect duties and is based on recognizition that we are all, at one time or another, in need of mutual assistance. Such an obligation is necessarily grounded in a compassion for others and for their suffering.

Entities of primary worth, on the other hand, may themselves be feared, loathed, and hated. Their destruction might greatly benefit many others and it may, in the final analysis, even be justified. But causing suffering to such an entity would have to be justified before doing so could be morally permissible. For example, in the case of a tyrant like Hitler, a hit man in Chicago, or a Bengal tiger raiding villages to eat children, an argument for harming that entity can be made, but such harm, to be morally acceptable, would have to be justified. One would at least have to show that (1) there was no other way than the one chosen to deal with the problem, (2) that allowing Hitler, the Chicago hit man, or the Bengal tiger to continue on their way would inevitably produce suffering not only in many others but in others whose primary worth was greater, and then (3) that the action chosen was not only one which would remove the threat but also that it was one which would cause the least suffering to Hitler, the Chicago hit man, or the Bengal tiger.

The value (or disvalue) of objects of secondary worth is either material or symbolic. Damaging a car matters because its material value to another may be great; the loss of a car or its use may inflict serious material damage. Belittling a religious symbol is harmful not for material but for symbolic reasons; spitting on the cross or denigrating the Torah may cause great suffering to a believer.

Harming objects of negative secondary worth usually does not need quite as elaborate justification as harming entities of primary worth. While objects of secondary worth are more often universally valued or disvalued this is by no means always the case. Material objects may be highly valued by one person and a great threat (and therefore greatly disvalued) by another. Assault rifles in the hands of a paramilitary group or atomic weapons held by a particular nation are but two obvious examples. Symbolic objects (take the Nazi flag, the hammer and sickle, or the ensignia of the KKK) may likewise have a great value for some and a great disvalue for others.

Objects may have both material and symbolic worth. Burning books matters both for material and for symbolic reasons. A book may be a valuable addition to my library or one which I have plans to sell, or it may symbolize freedom of thought to me and to my community. Furthermore, the material worth of an object may be great but its symbolic worth may be negative. A gold swastika which had been used in Nazi pageantry may serve as an example. On the other hand, the symbolic worth of an object may be fairly great but it may, materially speaking, be disvalued. A holy object or relic which carried and could spread infectious organisms would be an example.

Objects, furthermore, may have more than one kind of moral worth. A dog, in our framework, has primary worth: It has the capacity to suffer. It may, however, also be a particularly fine specimen of a particularly rare breed (or one of the few survivors of a threatened species and, therefore, irreplaceable). It, therefore, has secondary value in that losing the dog would not only cause its owner much grief but also some material loss. Such an animal, furthermore, may have been an especially treasured pet of the owner's deceased wife and, therefore and in addition to its material worth, have immeasurable symbolic value. Objects can at the same time have primary, secondary, and symbolic worth and they can have varying amounts of each. Using the notions of primary, secondary, and symbolic worth hardly lends itself to a cookie-cutting approach in which answers emerge ready made from the concept.

Dividing objects into categories of primary and secondary worth and subdividing secondary worth into material and symbolic worth is, of course, reminiscent of Kant. Kant speaks of the value of persons to whom we owe "respect" as well as of "market" and "affective" value.[1] These notions are quite similar to the notion of primary (respect), secondary (market), and symbolic (affective) worth. Kant, however, would claim that an object is deserving of respect only because it has the capacity for self-legislation and autonomous function. Grounding respect (or primary worth) in the capacity for self-legislation would leave out a large number of entities (the severely feebleminded or most animals, for example) which grounding moral concern in the capacity to suffer would not. In Kant's philosophy, our duties to entities incapable of self-legislation are derivable not from the entities themselves but are duties only because cruelty of any kind taints those deserving of respect.[2] Market or affective value, furthermore, is judgeable only on the terms of the valuing done by entities capable of self-legislation. A puppy's toy would have little moral standing.[3]

A few illustrations may serve. Physicians, consistent with their historical vision of the physician-patient relationship, are obligated to pursue their patients' good. How physicians define or have historically defined that good is another matter. But once and however defined, physicians are obligated to serve that good consistently regardless of peripheral considerations. A critically ill patient who wishes to live cannot be denied treatment because the family (or the hospital administrator) would like the physician to stop treatment. Let us take an example:

> Mr. Smith is a twenty-eight-year-old man who had a severe accident and who is now in precarious shape in the ICU. There is only a slim chance that he will survive. Several other patients in the same hospital are waiting for organ transplantation and, as it happens, they all match with Mr. Smith. Mr. Smith's family, furthermore, asks that the physician do nothing more so that the organs can be transplanted. Mr. Smith is poor and carries no insurance. The hospital administrator urges that no more be done both because of Mr. Smith's inability to pay and because his bed is needed by other patients who can pay.

At this point, Mr. Smith continues to be of primary moral worth. He is not beyond hope, he still has the potential for suffering and, therefore, his interest within the context of the patient-physician relationship takes precedence. Classically, no matter what the wishes of the family or the needs of deserving others, efforts to return Mr. Smith to a meaningful life must continue. As an entity of primary worth within the context of the patient-physician relationship, Mr. Smith classically and practically remains at center stage.

Things are, however, not quite that simple when it comes to situations in which satisfactory recovery to a sentient state no longer remains a possibility. Using the capacity to suffer as a framework for making such decisions forces us to consider some of the problems posed when surrogates must try to separate their own interests from the interests of permanently and severely mentally impaired patients.[4] Classically, surrogates are to consider only the interest of the patient in whose stead they act. When, however, decisions about patients barely capable of suffering and certainly no longer capable of deriving pleasure are to be made, a framework of suffering (the surrogate's as well as the patient's) may at times allow an analysis far different than the one conventionally used.[5]

> Several days have elapsed since Mr. Smith still had a fair chance for satisfactory recovery. He is now on a ventilator and, according to reliable criteria, is found to be brain dead. At this point the family who have been talking it over are inclining against allowing organ donation. Furthermore, the hospital administrator, especially since the patient cannot pay, continues to want the use of the ICU bed.

The issue now is quite different. Brain dead or permanently vegetative persons no longer are entities of primary worth: Their neocortex and their limbic system are beyond repair, their capacity to suffer no longer exists, and, therefore, they cannot now or in the future suffer. The physician's obligation, therefore, is considerably changed. Other considerations than those narrowly dealing with Mr. Smith's biological existence legitimately move to center stage. Mr. Smith now has secondary worth: His organs are of material value to prospective recipients, his presence in the ICU is disvalued by the hospital administrator, and his body has symbolic worth for both family and community. No longer is the person Mr. Smith at center stage; other considerations may legitimately enter in.

Such considerations grounded in an entities capacity to suffer are inevitably intertwined with notions of "animal rights."[6,7] If one grants higher animals—those with a neocortex and a limbic system however primitive—primary moral standing, one would need to justify the use of animals for the sake of humans be it as articles of food, clothing, or as subjects of experimentation. From our vantage point there is clearly a moral difference between an intelligent parakeet and a college student, or between a severely retarded person who is incapable of contact with the environment and an intelligent chimpanzee. In sorting out hierarchies of value, some attention will have to be paid to this.

When we speak of the capacity to suffer we are not yet ready to affirm that the depth of that capacity endows objects with higher or lower relative standing. Merely having that capacity now or in the future gives such an entity primary worth and, therefore, standing as an object of direct moral concern. Such standing, however, forms only a basis for consideration and not the sufficient ground for the eventual judgment. Entities which have the capacity to suffer have a prima facie claim against being made to suffer, but such a claim is far from absolute. Things are rarely as clear cut as they were with Mr. Smith.

When we judge among competing entities, all of whom are of primary worth, choices need to be made. Such choices inevitably will favor a lesser wrong rather than being between a right and a wrong choice. In ethics as in most decisions generally, the choice between what is perceived as good or right and what is seen to be bad or wrong is relatively easy. Rarely do people deliberately and knowingly choose the overall "bad" rather than the overall "good." Inevitably the conflict is between similar but not quite equally attractive or similar but not quite equally repulsive possibilities.[5]

In making moral decisions we frequently have to choose an act which in itself and seen outside its context is bad. Breaking a promise to keep a dinner date because we had to stop to help an injured person is undoubtedly a correct choice. Helping the injured is, in this instance, a stronger compulsion than not breaking a dinner date. And while helping the injured person was a right thing to do, and while it certainly explains or even excuses the breaking of the previous promise, it does not make promise breaking (seen by itself) a right act. Praiseworthy as helping an injured person is, the blameworthiness of promise breaking is thereby not expunged. Rather, the blameworthiness is outflanked and overpowered. The actor is praiseworthy for helping a person in distress, praiseworthy for making the correct choice (and, especially, for weighing options and sometimes agonizing over them before choosing), but a residuum of blameworthiness remains. Assuming blameworthiness does not necessitate "beating oneself." Rather it is an acknowledgment that, try as we may, we were forced to do a wrong. Such an assumption of blameworthiness, if seen in the proper light, can well serve as a prod to moral growth and learning. Perhaps next time things could be done a little differently: a message sent, an apology given.[5]

In making choices among competing objects of moral worth, a similar situation pertains. We may be able to justify causing suffering, we may be able to show why Hitler, the Chicago hit man, or the Bengal tiger must be shot, (but not why they should be tortured to death) but causing suffering (or killing) can never be seen as praiseworthy in itself. Perhaps next time the problem occurs a better and more humane solution can be found (Hitler or the Chicago hit man may be captured and imprisoned; the Bengal tiger may be shot with a tranquilizer and taken to a zoo).

When we fail to assume blameworthiness and claim that our action of promise breaking or killing was good, we may feel better about it; but we cannot learn. Next time the problem occurs we will do the same thing as before: There is little reason why, if we look at what we did as the right thing to do, we should search for a better way.

Changing blameworthiness to praiseworthiness, instead of simply acknowledging that under the circumstances our blameworthy act was still better than the alternative, is not a prod but a hindrance to moral growth and learning. Such a move puts our moral sensitivities to rest. Our natural compassion and pity instead of being guided by reason is overpowered by rationalization and smothered by self-proclaimed righteousness.

Delineating hierarchies of value so that moral judgment can proceed attempts to assign differing values to entities, all of whom have moral standing. While delineating such hierarchies may help us make difficult choices, it does not, in any situation, remove moral standing from those adjudged to have lesser standing. When we must choose to cause suffering to one rather than to another, and when we do so according to basic criteria and in fulfillment of communal values, we remain, unfortunately, blameworthy. And, hopefully, acknowledging blameworthiness may help us find a better way which failure to acknowledge blameworthiness might easily conceal.

When, as an example, we use mice in experiments to find a cure for a terrible human disease and assume that doing so is morally neutral or even that it is praiseworthy, no prod to finding a different way exists. If, however, we allow our pity and compassion for the suffering of others to enter the equation, and, stimulated by this, we acknowledge and are troubled by our blameworthiness, things may have a different outcome. We now regretfully acknowledge that there is a hierarchy which places the human species above the rodent, but we also come to realize that the existence of such a hierarchy hardly makes causing suffering in rodents morally neutral or praiseworthy. Such a realization stimulates us to keep such suffering to a minimum and, above all, to search for better ways. We may discover that computer models, the use of a lower species with a lesser capacity to suffer or, perhaps, tissue cultures would serve equally well.

Delineating hierarchies (whether hierarchies among objects of primary or secondary worth or adjudicating between a low primary and a high secondary value) is neither simple nor permanent. It is an ongoing quest which takes place in the embrace of evolving communal values and which is subject to learning and growth. We may find that the categories we delineate today do not serve us tomorrow and that, therefore, new categories or new nuances of distinction between entities are needed. More understanding in the biological or behavioral sciences may show us that our concept of suffering, or our understanding of who can and who cannot suffer and to what extent, was naive and untenable. (For example—unlikely as it seems—we could learn that amoebas have a heretofore undiscovered organelle which substitutes for the neocortex and limbic system in higher organisms.) Or social sensitivities may evolve so that a far richer notion of suffering or a differing vision of what makes entities suffer emerges. (For example, as living standards change our vision of what our fellows need to prevent their suffering may undergo drastic changes.) We view the ritual infant sacrifice by the Babylonian peasant as wrong by today's light even though the equally human and aware Babylonian peasantry viewed it as right in their age. The rite is not changed, but our understanding of what it entails and our capacity for compassion and hence our social sensitivity (which, after all, influences our vision of personal morality) have evolved.

Inevitably, when we delineate hierarchies of primary moral worth, we have to adjudicate between entities, all of whom have moral standing in themselves. They all enjoy a prima facie claim against being made to suffer and we have an obligation not to cause wanton suffering to such entities. If it is at all possible to set such hierarchies (if, in other words, a method of evaluating worth external to the evaluator is to be found) some method of making such very difficult choices needs to be developed. This, of course, gets to the very issue of why it is that life in any form should be of value.

The vitalist will claim that all life is precious by virtue of being life. This is usually framed in the religious terms of sanctity. It is, furthermore, a claim which is made almost universally for human life alone; were it otherwise the person who made and held to such a claim would inevitably starve. People who make this claim must, if they are to be consistent, oppose the termination of treatment or the writing of "do not resuscitate" orders under any and all circumstances. Vitalists who might subscribe to an ethic based on the capacity to suffer would, by the same token, give all entities with that capacity equal standing. Vitalists hold life (or might, perhaps, hold the capacity to suffer) as an absolute good. In everyday life, and especially among health professionals who daily have to deal with pain and suffering, there are few vitalists. For the sake of this work, I shall largely ignore the vitalist position because it affronts experience and moral sensitivity and because it locks us into an inflexible and untenable position. All biological existence (even all human biological existence) cannot be preserved: no one seriously proposes, for example, the preservation of all human tissue cultures, and yet cultures of human tissue are most certainly alive and most assuredly human. All suffering (even all human suffering), likewise, cannot be prevented.

If we discount the vitalist position and do not advance the claim that life is a good in itself, we must then seek to discover when and under what circumstances life does constitute a good. In such a view, life is an instrumental good, good because it serves as a condition for the attainment of other goods. Life, in such a point of view, far from being a good in itself, is the necessary condition for experience. The nonvitalist position, rather than focusing on biological life, inevitably focuses on the nature of the experience. Maintaining life serves to underwrite the possibility of experience, good or bad.

It is the nature and depth of experience which helps us to determine whether we consider our lives worthwhile. There is no doubt that to the individual who is the subject of his only life, it is under ordinary circumstances, immeasurably precious. Seen from inside that particular life, no other measure can be applied. But that does not mean that, seen from the outside, all can benefit equally from having a life.[6] When we must make hard choices, say choices between hopelessly demented patients and college students, or between sparrows and gorillas, some external standard needs to be applied. If this cannot be done, no choices can be made and since, inevitably, they must be made, they will be based on caprice or whim. Rolling the dice to determine which of these conflicting pairs is to be injured or is to die when one inevitably must, denies moral agency by the claim that there are no morally relevant differences. The questions of what is and what is not a morally relevant difference, and why difference is morally relevant constitutes the moral quandary.

Under some circumstances nonhuman animals may well have far higher moral standing then do members of the human species. Permanently vegetative persons, for example, cannot be said to have primary moral worth albeit that they retain both symbolic and material secondary worth. Chimpanzees, dogs, and guinea pigs who can suffer certainly have primary worth although (as I shall argue, by virtue of their lesser capacity to self-legislate, formulate hopes, and have aspirations) their primary worth under normal circumstances may be less than that of a member of the human species. Permanently vegetative persons (or anencephalis infants), therefore, derive their moral standing purely by virtue of their secondary moral worth. It is this secondary moral worth which, in case of moral conflict, must be balanced against the primary worth of functionally intact members of a "lower" species.[7]

When we focus on the nature of experience which entities of primary worth have, differences do emerge. Being alive is important only because it makes having a life possible. Having a life is the sum total of our history, hopes, aspirations, and social interconnections; it is the rich skein of our biography past, present, and future. The richness of our biographies matters no less than the fact that we are alive. Such a point of view, however, has obvious dangers. First of all, it necessitates a prior judgment that greater or lesser richness is morally relevant. Secondly, it suffers from the necessity of an external standard that judges what is and what is not rich and that inevitably will choose on its own terms. Thirdly, it inevitably introduces the danger of a slippery slope and opens a Pandora's box of unsavory possibilities. We are, it seems, caught between an absolute straight jacket of valuing purely on the terms of the valuer, and thus locking ourselves into an untenable position, or opening the door to a dangerous situation.

In making a judgment that it is the greater or lesser richness of a life that matters, we are advancing the claim that people with richer lives, richer plans, and a richer capacity for experiencing have a greater stake in their lives than do people whose lives are less complex. Such a claim has obvious dangers. It threatens to make a lower order of people whose lives are impoverished, whose plans—because of a lack of talent or opportunity—have been foreshortened, and who because of a lack of education have a smaller capacity for experience. If one were to take such a claim literally one would, for example, hold that a homeless person with few plans or hopes for the future or a person unschooled and, therefore, incapable of enjoying the finer things in life had a smaller moral worth than did one living in a fine house, having elaborate plans for the future, and well versed in the arts. Such a claim is not what I have in mind. The person living an impoverished life has the same capacity for enjoying a richer life, has the same capacity for making future plans, and for profiting from experiences as does the other. Above all, such a person with an equal basic capacity for suffering is, in fact, suffering at this very time. Far from having a lesser value, therefore, such a person may even take priority because her present suffering could well be ameliorated easily. When I come to speak about a just community based in part on the notion of suffering, the duty to ameliorate the suffering of such persons will form a part of my argument.

Judging what is and what is not rich suffers from the necessity of an external standard of richness. It is, in a sense, the old story of "pushpins and poetry" which troubled Bentham's hedonistic calculus. When I speak of richness, I am not as much addressing content as I am speaking about the complexity of form. Humans with an innate capacity to plan their lives, to profit from the lessons of history, or to plot their future intuitively have a different standing than do creatures lacking such a capacity. The reason for this may, among other things, be the probability that the depth of capacity to suffer is related to such factors: Beings with a greater capacity to plan, with a better capacity to know the past and sense the future, will be able to experience suffering beyond pain more readily than those lacking such a capacity.

The slippery slope argument is often heard and it certainly is one which cannot be readily dismissed. Slippery slopes, it is said, are dangerous and must be avoided. Many unavoidable choices, however, entail the possibility of stepping onto a slippery slope. When I have a glass of wine with a good dinner, I risk a slippery slope: It may be the first step towards drunkenness or gluttony. Whatever we do, personally, professionally, or socially carries certain risks. Taking risks is an unavoidable part of life. Knowing that there is a risk does not ordinarily stop us from risk taking but rather causes us to try and minimize the risk, makes us more cautious, and causes us to pursue our tasks hedged by restrictions appropriate to the risk. Knowing the danger of a slippery slope, knowing that our action today may cause a cascade of worse actions tomorrow, should cause us to exert extreme caution and should force us to take pause. We must seek to provide as many safeguards as possible, but the mere mention of a slippery slope must not freeze us into inaction. There are few things—the manufacture of atomic weapons may be one—that are so inherently dangerous and so lack all reasonable content of desirability as to be better precluded altogether.[8] It is here that acknowledging our blameworthiness may help. Doing something we claim is fine prompts the next action and extends the notion of permissibility further. It helps us ignore the slippery slope and, therefore, helps our descent down it. The presence and the steepness of slippery slopes should counsel us to be wary, to examine carefully and to continue evaluating our actions both before and after we have taken them. But the presence of a slippery slope need not merely by its presence argue against a judgment or action, and the steepness of the slope can help determine the appropriate amount of wariness with which we approach it.

It is not at all clear that in delineating hierarchies of primary worth other factors may not also and quite properly enter in. Even when some persons may seem to have a lesser capacity for life plans and experiences, they are still human persons and, therefore, have a different symbolic value than do other beings. (Since we are humans, other humans have a greater symbolic value for us.) Basically such an argument still presupposes the dominance of the human species over all others and rests on the evident and troublesome claim that humans, by virtue of that power, have the right to make decisions of worth for others. A weak argument in support of such a claim might be the evident fact that humans, under current circumstances, are the only creatures capable of making such choices. Since such choices must be made, humans are the ones to make them and, inevitably, humans will favor their own species. Such an argument is troublesome and certainly deserves a great deal of careful attention. But it is not an argument which can be defended or refuted here. For the time being I will presume the argument to be true that humans alone can make such choices, that such choices must be made and that, therefore, they will inevitably favor the human species. Such a realization, just as the realization that we are about to embark on a slippery slope, should make us wary and should cause us to examine the judgments we make and the actions we take in that light.

When it comes to determining hierarchies of primary worth, then, the richness of the biography may well count as one factor. A claim that the richness of a sparrow's life is less than that of a college student's can easily be advanced and successfully defended. Another and perhaps at least as important consideration, may be the Kantian notion of self-legislation: Entities capable of enunciating their own law may be given a higher standing than entities without such a capacity. Enunciating one's own moral law is part of a person's biography and contributes to its richness. Such notions, of course, offer severe problems. If the richness of one's biography is what matters (or at least the capacity to have such a richness) and if the capacity for self-legislation is another factor, does that not inevitably reduce the moral standing of the less intelligent, or the less sensitive? Such an obvious danger can be hedged by a social decision that all humans capable of sentient life (by virtue of their innately higher capacity even if not by virtue of their individual higher function) take precedence over other organisms. Whether such a decision is or is not ultimately defensible, or whether it should or should not be made, is not the issue. The point is that somewhere along the line morally sensitive communities will have to be engaged in making decisions which, inevitably, will have some arbitrary component. It is at this point of personal morality that the nature and structure of community, which forms the subject of later considerations in this book, first becomes crucial. Communities, I will argue, form the seedbed of personal morality.

Whenever lines are drawn, gray zones persist. This is as true of science as it is of morality. Ultimately the decision to call a given lab value "normal" and another "abnormal" (and thus deciding that any particular patient falls inside or outside the range of normal) is arbitrary. No one, however, would seriously suggest that just because gray zones persist, diagnoses or decisions should not be made. Gray zones, like slippery slopes, merely counsel discernment and discretion and necessitate more due care (and the consideration of other factors) in

making a particular judgment. When it comes to making moral judgments, we must use discernment and discretion rather than refuse to
make judgments).

Carving out rational categories of this sort may help. Saying that
something has more and another less worth, however, does not suffice.
Just because the life plan of a cow is arguably less rich than that of a college student or because cows are incapable of self-legislation does not
of itself excuse the eating of hamburgers. The injunction against causing others to suffer has to be overridden by weighty considerations.
Preserving the integrity of entities of higher moral worth would be
such a consideration; pleasing their palates would not. One can live and
live very well without eating meat; eating meat is not necessary to pre-
serve either physical or spiritual integrity. On the other hand, one cannot, or cannot very well, live without curing disease. Therefore, with
severe hedges and careful restrictions, the use of some animals in medical experiments has a different standing than the use of animals for
food.

Secondary worth is attributed to an object (material or not)
according to the value which entities of primary worth have for it. This
gives a certain proxy moral standing to cars, houses, ideas, and beliefs.
Since the worth of such an object and, therefore, the regard in which it
should be held, depends upon its worth to one who values it, it follows
that our concern depends upon the particular worth we invest in the
valuer. Objects valued by college students are, therefore, generally but
not always of more concern than objects valued by sparrows. Once
again, it depends upon the reason for valuing: An object needed to pre-
serve the life of a sparrow but wanted for the transient amusement of a
college student has a quite different standing than would an object
needed either for the life or the amusement of both.

In trying to formulate hierarchies, I do not suggest either that primary worth inevitably overrides secondary nor that hierarchies are
fixed and immutable. Something may have incredible secondary worth
and protecting such a value may entail causing suffering or destroying
a being of primary worth. Crops needed to feed a village and devas-
tated by a swarm of birds or a precious painting threatened by a swarm
of rodents may be examples. Even in such cases, however, such entities
(which are still of primary worth) need to be treated with all consideration due to them. Killing such creatures leaves us blameworthy and
acknowledging such blameworthiness (not making a good thing out of
a thing we know to be bad) may prompt us to seek better solutions:
Perhaps devices to keep away the birds or ways of trapping and then
releasing the rodents can be found.

In this brief discussion, I do not want to enter fully into the morass of the abortion debate. Let me show in a few paragraphs, however, how my argument applies. To give primary moral standing only to entities capable of suffering would leave out entities in the process of becoming (embryos) as well as entities whose being is temporarily suspended (the impermanently unconscious or anaesthetized). For that reason and since, rather obviously, there is a difference between such entities and those of secondary, symbolic, or no moral worth, some attention must be paid to them. Those who find abortion categorically and under all circumstances impermissible must do so on a moral sense peculiar to their particular belief system. Claiming that no morally relevant differences exist between a gastrula and the mother carrying that gastrula is to make a claim which can be defended only by an appeal to a belief system taking authority as its basis. Reason by itself cannot uphold such a claim. A viewpoint of this sort is similar to one which would advance the claim that once primary worth is attained, no further differentiation between the claimants is possible. Other attributes of the claimant beyond the fact of being a claimant do not matter: Once having secured a place in court, a necessary judgment follows.

The argument distinguishing the unborn from unconscious or anaesthetized persons is brief. Such persons have a neocortex and limbic system, have a biography and, therefore, already have a stake in their existence and in their continuity. Holding them to be of no moral concern merely because their activity is suspended does not make sense. Claiming that they, once unconscious or anaesthetized, can have no further claim to primary worth is analogous to claiming that one is free to rob a house once the owner has left for the day. The unborn have a different standing. Theirs is not a claim advanced on the basis of personal history. At least early on, they lack a neocortex and a limbic system and even for a time after the formation of the system it is nonfunctional and empty. Fetuses, at least early in their development, lack even the most rudimentary biography or life plans. Their claim is potential: It may be the case that they will have a biography and develop a life plan and, after the fact, they will have had an interest in being born. But while considerations of this sort give fetuses moral standing, it is a different kind of moral standing than is the moral standing of their mothers. It is the moral standing of generic property before personal ownership has been established. Taking it is certainly not morally neutral but it is different than robbing a house while the owner is gone.

Early on the worth of the fetus is secondary: It has material value to the parents who want a child (or is disvalued by those who do not) as well as symbolic value to the parents and to the community. Its primary worth is potential and unrealized. That does not make its value trivial but it makes its value a different one than the value enjoyed by an actual being. Fetuses, furthermore, may have a potential for terrible suffering: They may be the subjects of painful and crippling diseases relentlessly driving them to an agonizing postpartum death. When such things can be foretold, one could argue that such fetuses have an interest in not being allowed to suffer, indeed that they have an interest in not being born. Such considerations do not begin to come to grips with the abortion issue but they suggest that it is fallacious to simply claim that since the fetus has potential primary worth it must be treated as though its primary worth were actualized and complete.

Notions of moral worth, how we deal with choosing between conflicting entities, and the way we perceive community necessarily intertwine to produce what we call our sense of obligation. Our moral sense, as well as our sense of compassion, is deeply rooted in the way our minds are structured as well as being created by our social nexus. The raw material (the form) of our minds with their common structure is shaped into our particular morality by the social nexus in which we exist. To have an obligation is to feel more or less compelled to do something. Moral obligation necessitates freedom. Not absolute freedom in the sense that we are totally free but freedom within biological and social constraints. Without such elbow room the very notion of obligation is incoherent.[9] In turn, sentient beings shape and explore this freedom and create visions of moral possibilities. I have briefly argued that one aspect of creating visions of moral possibility is to discover the ground notion of what leads us to have moral concern for some but not for other things. In the present chapter I have not so much given hierarchies of moral worth as suggested that the carving out of such hierarchies is an ongoing one in which all must participate and from which all must learn. In the chapters to come, I shall explore the social nexus so important to our formulation and finally emerge with a notion of how communities and individuals can fruitfully and to the benefit of each interact.

## References

1. Kant I: *Grundlegung zur Metaphysik der Sitten*. Leipzig: Felix Meiner Verlag, 1925.

2. Kant I: Duties towards Animals and Spirits. In *Immanuel Kant Lectures on*

*Ethics*, L. Infield, trans. Gloucester, MA: Peter Smith, 1978.

3. Loewy EH: Suffering, Moral Worth and Medical Ethics: A New Beginning. *Bridges* 1(3/4):103-17, 1989.

4. Hardwig J: What about the Family? *Hastings Center Reporter* 20(2):5-10, 1990.

5. Singer P: *Animal Liberation*. New York: Random House, 1975.

6. Regan T, Singer P: *Animal Rights and Human Obligation*. Englewood Cliffs, NJ: Prentice-Hall, 1976.

7. Loewy EH: The Role of Suffering and Community in Medical Ethics. *J Med Ethics* 1(2), 1990 (in publication).

8. Loewy EH: *Textbook of Medical Ethics*. New York: Plenum Publishers, 1989.

9. Rachels J: *The End of Life*. New York: Oxford University Press, 1986.

10. Loewy EH: Drunks, Livers and Values: Should Social Value Judgments Enter into Liver Transplant Decisions? *J Chin Gastroenterol* 9(4):436-41, 1987.

11. Dennet DC: *Elbow Room: The Varieties of Free Will Worth Having*. Cambridge: MIT Press, 1985.

# Chapter Four

# Social Contract, Community Structure, and Obligation*

The way we perceive our obligations to others is shaped by the kind of community in which we live. What we consider to be of moral worth, the things we consider to be moral or nonmoral questions (if such a differentiation can really be clearly made) all are conditioned by community. In turn, the way we look at community, its structure, its obligations to us and ours to it, all depend upon the way we feel about social contract. This chapter is devoted to exploring the shaping of social contract, to how the idea of social contract underpins our conceptions of community and, in turn, how our perception of obligations emerges from this.

Even when they differ about the nature of obligations, moral agents—by virtue of being moral agents—will acknowledge that obligations exist. The fact that inclinations may conflict with what we perceive to be our obligations, likewise, comes as no surprise: if this were not the case the very term "obligation," except as it might be used to describe cause in a mechanical sense, would not be truly meaningful. Obligation suggests that there may be a conflict either between what we want to do and what we feel we ought to do, or between different but mutually contradictory obligations. Obligation, except when used in a mechanistic causal sense, necessitates freedom. Freedom is not an absolute, we are constrained by biological as well as by social forces, but it is freedom

---

*The beginning of this chapter is derived largely from two sources: a paper entitled "Obligations, Community and Suffering: Problems of Community Seen in a New Light" and published in *Bridges* 2(1/2):1-16, 1990, and one entitled "Social Contract, Communities and Guardians" which appeared in the *Journal of Elder Abuse and Neglect* 2(3/4):123-124, 1990.

which allows us the latitude to maneuver within such a framework. It is the very real elbow room we have and without which obligation is incoherent.[1]

To have an obligation is to feel more or less compelled to do something. Compulsion, in that sense, is adherence (voluntary or otherwise) to what is or what is perceived to be a law. Generally, when an object follows a strict physical law, we do not use the language of obligation: We do not say that an egg dropped to the floor is compelled to break but rather that it is bound to do so. At bottom, the term compulsion and the term obligation share a common meaning. We are compelled to breathe, not only if we want to live but even if we do not want to live: Apocryphal stories to the contrary, under normal conditions holding one's breath until one dies is made impossible by a variety of nonvoluntary reflexes. On the other hand, we can refrain from eating despite our biological drive to do so and, therefore, can starve ourselves to death. Such an obligation to take fluids and nutrition can be opposed by an act of will. In the same way we can refrain from killing our enemy even when every desire prompts us to do so and even when the circumstances in which we find ourselves are such that no one need know that we have committed murder. An act of will, obeying what we perceive to be a higher law, acts as a brake. It is a higher law which supplies the internal compulsion overcoming our natural desire.

Kant terms this higher law "duty": the thing or things that one is expected to do.[2] It is this sense of duty (or of obligation) that he juxtaposes against inclination: We may be inclined to do something (lie, steal, or murder) or we may be inclined to refrain from doing something (help our neighbor); it is duty which acts in opposition to inclination. In Kant's view, duty and inclination are not two arms of a dialectic: they do not vie with each other until a synthesis is found. Rather, duty has moral veto power: Whether inclination prompts for or against it, ethical behavior has little to do with following our inclination but consists, at least in the usual interpretation of Kant, of opposing inclination and doing things merely out of a sense of duty. It is the ability to formulate one's own rational duty (to make autonomous rules) which, in Kant's viewpoint, sets man apart, and in Kant's system it is this capacity which endows persons with primary worth and makes it illicit to use others merely as means towards a given end. In the human condition (but not for what Kant posits as the Divine Being) there is an inevitable and inherent dualism between duty and inclination.

Prior to Kant, obligation was not as clearly formulated. It was implicit, however, not only in the Greek philosophers but perhaps at least as significantly in the early Greek dramatists. *Antigone* is nothing but a struggle between obedience to the law of a temporal ruler and obedience to a higher law.[3] Likewise, the story of Homer's *Odyssey* revolves around sometimes conflicting obligations and duties.[4]

A teleological framework accepts as obligatory those actions serving an ultimate good. The highest good, in such an ethic, is the source of obligation but what the highest good may be is variously understood. Socrates, Plato and Aristotle all identify individual with social good and ethical actions achieve such a good: For Plato, the tendency toward a "form" or universal model of the Good; for Aristotle the achievement of goals towards which humans naturally aim.[5,6] To thinkers in the medieval period, the ultimate good is union with God, the source of all moral values.[7] On this perspective, the community is a community of believers who together strive for such a union. Obligation is the obligation to conform to God's (or nature's) law. Such a point of view is reflected in today's "natural law" theorists who hold obligation to be conformity to natural (or God's) law.

Utilitarians in general will tie obligation to a vision of the good. Acts (or rules) likely to achieve the greatest good for the greatest number carry more weight than others bringing about a lesser good or, perhaps, resulting in evil.[8] This, of course, leaves the good undefined. Intuitionists, on the other hand, have felt that the entire enterprise is flawed: What is and what is not right is evident to us. Rationality can only help by giving us insight into our intuitive behavior and can delineate the wellsprings of human interests which give rise to our intuitions. But reason, or at least reason alone, cannot justify our obligations.[9]

All of these theories would seem to have obligation rooted in a sense of the self. The question, "what ought I to do," is basic to any problem of obligation. A sense of the self, however, is basically a social sense incoherent outside the social nexus in which it occurs. Selves, apart from community, are unintelligible: even hermits who to become hermits have left their community define themselves in communal terms. For this and many other reasons, it is not possible to reduce the problem of obligation to individual choice or to make of communal obligation a mathematically determined individual voting process. As John Dewey so clearly saw, a basic theory of obligation necessitates a concrete relation to a moral end and moral ends are socially determined.[10,11]

The idea of obligation connects individual with communal ethics. A sense of obligation has two roots and two faces. It is nourished by our idea of individual relationships with specific others as well as by our notion of ourselves in community, and it is sustained by our notion of ourselves in community. Obligation is manifest in our dealings with

specific individuals and in our relationships within and with community. These two roots and faces, however, are not separate but are themselves intertwined and interrelated. Our sense of obligation towards
specific others develops in the embrace of community and our experience in the way we relate to others in turn shapes our perception and
eventually the way we structure community. Saying that individual
ethics is more easily dealt with by using considerations of deontology,
autonomy, and freedom whereas communal ethics is more reflective of
utilitarian considerations is superficially true but creates a dualism in
which communal and individual considerations are seen as inherently
separate and separable. Although, as we shall argue, there is a dialectic
relationship between the community and the individual, it must be recognized that these two limbs are neither entirely separate nor strictly
separable, that, in fact, they are unavoidably attached to each other. The
relationship between the individual and the community of which he
partakes is based on fundamental assumptions about communities and
their structure. Fundamental assumptions about community, in turn,
derive from the way in which we look at social contract.

The existence of social contract will be assumed rather than
argued for. If one means by social contract an association of persons
coming together in order to govern themselves, one is talking of a
somewhat different matter than what will be meant here. Government
can be the result of social contract but not all or even most governments
are. Some are the result of an assumption of power by small groups acting merely for their own narrow self-interest and ready to ignore their
social roots. Such governments may maintain themselves by force or
stealth for a historical "little while" but in a historical sense they cannot
truly endure.

Social contract, while it may be used more narrowly to support
various forms of government, is a far richer concept than merely the
concept underwriting government: It implies all the tacit agreements
ultimately enabling communal life. A wider social contract, in turn,
enables the formation of such associations in the first place.[12-14] Social
contract implies those unspoken, tacit assumptions which meld people
together and which allow them to exist as associations. It consists, in
other words, of those things which "go without saying."[15] A collective
or community of any size is not possible without such fundamental and
quite tacit understandings. Government, and ultimately law, emerges
from social contract and in turn government and law may influence the
evolution of the way we look at social contract and obligation. Since
social contract and obligation and government and law profoundly
influence each other, the relationship is eventually reciprocal, but gov-

ernment and law are ontologically subsequent and not prior to the contract itself. Life in any association without a social contract—life without such tacit understandings and eventually undertakings whatever they might be in the particular—would be unimaginable.

The idea of social contract has been used by all sides to argue for their positions. Conventional assumptions of the old testament as well as the beliefs of the early Christian and later Catholic and Protestant churches relied on notions of social contract. Tyrants used their particular ideas of social contract to justify their claims to power and social contract theory underwrote the pleadings of Locke and Jefferson for democratic government. Marxist theory relied on social agreement and ultimately the idea of social contract underwrote the Marxist vision of a classless society. Capitalists used a particular vision of social contract to support their insistence on individualism and autonomy to the neglect of beneficence and other virtues.

If it is the case that social contract has or can be used to underwrite man's vision of contradictory things, what credibility can the notion of social contract have and of what use can it be? To this question there are a number of responses. In the first place, the fact that an object or idea can be used to bring about evil (or what we perceive to be evil) does not necessarily speak against it; it merely shows wrong usage and counsels caution. Secondly, it can be argued that some of the specific visions of social contract rather than the very idea of the existence of such a contract are flawed. In short, the problems are substantive rather than conceptual.

The question of ontological priority, the question of whether communities spawn individuals or whether individuals voluntarily associate to produce communities, is one often raised. When man first originated, some will argue, individuals lived their lonely lives constantly threatened by others. Life was as Hobbes says, "solitary, nasty, brutish and short." It is often claimed that the very notion of social contract implies the ontological priority of the individual since words such as "free association" or "tacit agreements" imply individuals who freely associate or agree. On the other hand, others will maintain that early human existence necessarily started in associations and that individuals and the realization of individual existence emerged from such associations. Agreement and association, while fundamentally an agreement and association of individual persons, cannot simply be reduced to an ahistorical association or agreement of individuals. I shall have cause to examine these assumptions as we go along.

Notions of social contract are not new. The fact of social contract itself, as distinct from governmental contract, is so very evident and

obvious that it may often be missed because it is tacitly assumed.
Hebrew society presumed a social contract which governed its laws
and which was even reflected in the covenant Jews sought with God.
The notion is evident in the Greek polis and expressed in Plato's *Republic*. It weaves through much of Cicero and Roman law. During the middle ages, Christianity assumed a social contract which united all members of the community whatever their rank and such notions could and
were used to justify serfdom. The mutual obligations of the feudal system assumed mutual obligations and understandings and were the fertile field in which later notions of social contract flourished. It is not by
accident that the Magna Carta of 1215 took mutual obligations among
all members of society for granted, rather than isolating the sovereign
by making him responsible only to God. Social contract, as a device to
argue for and ultimately to bring about democratic governments and
institutions, has ancient roots.

The idea of social contract (at least as it is heard by modern ears)
carries with it a notion of equality. As the seventeenth-century English
Leveller Colonel Rainsborough wrote:

> Really, I think that the poorest he that is in England has a life to
> live as the greatest he: and, therefore, truly Sir I think it's clear that
> every man . . . ought first by his own consent to put himself under
> that government.[14]

About the same time, Hobbes vigorously argued for—rather than tacitly assuming—the first modern notion of social contract. Definitely
assuming that ontological priority of the individual, Hobbes saw original man as living in the "state of nature" a life that was "solitary, nasty,
brutish and short."[16] In such a Hobbesian state of nature, persons were
afraid to come upon others who were as likely as not to kill, injure, or
rob them. They lived a life of fear and it is this pervasive fear of one
another which, Hobbes claims, gave the impetus for the original contract. If fear of each other could be reduced and men could be reasonably free of fear from their fellows, a more productive life for all would
result. And so, in the original Hobbesian state of nature, men came out
from behind their trees or rocks to covenant with each other and, ultimately, to reach a compact predicated merely on mutual nonharm. All
were free to pursue their own lives and activities as long as those pursuits did not actively infringe upon the life and activity of their fellows.
Coming to their fellows' aid was not part of such a compact: Not harming each other was all that was required. To ensure compliance, a
sovereign had to be given all power except the power to kill (without

justification) his subjects. Life, under such conditions, was seen to be more peaceful and pursuing one's own interests was thought a good deal safer.[16]

Even if one presumes individuals to have ontological priority to communities, there are other ways than Hobbes's of thinking about social contract. Locke saw social contract as an association of equally free men united by an evolving trust ("trust" in a quasi-legalistic sense) rather than as a contract based merely on mutual fear. In order to take such a contract seriously, natural law, resting ultimately on God's will, had to be assumed. Executing (and formulating) the laws is the duty of the individual rather than merely the function of an omnipotent sovereign. Locke's "state of nature" was quite different from the warlike state Hobbes had envisioned and men had come together for far different reasons than terror alone.[17] To both Hobbes and Locke individuals were ontologically prior to community and freedom for Hobbes as well as for Locke remained (almost) an absolute. These ideas underwrote the later concepts of Jefferson and may have played their part in some of the notions subsequently developed by Adam Smith.

Rousseau took this entire concept a good deal further. For him, the state of nature was considerably more primitive than was Locke's (which, curiously, included such notions as private property and an economy), but for Rousseau primitive life was more benign and not endowed with the same savageness as it had been for Hobbes. Primitive man was essentially an isolated and amoral being, a being, however, already and by nature endowed with a "natural sense of pity." In Rousseau's view, social structure originates in the general will which emerges through the establishment of civil associations and is "constant, incorruptible and pure."[18] Social structure created individual morality by transforming the amoral and animal-like state of nature.[18] To Rousseau, just as for Hobbes and quite in contrast to "natural law" conceptions of social contract, the social contract could occur only after some development of the primitive state had occurred. Prior to the possibility of a social contract, human character had to be changed. Individuals, it seems, were still decidedly prior to community.

As Rousseau envisioned social contract, individuals can only be properly seen within the nexus of their social connections. Associations of this sort, just as is the case with Locke, do far more than merely prevent mutual harm: They actively promote the good, here seen as a social good incomprehensible outside the social nexus. To Rousseau the condition of "civilized man," in which poverty and injustice were the rule, violated the original contract and ran counter to the general will. A return to a more basic way of life, like that prior to corruption, was to be desired.

Individuals (most emphatically as seen by Hobbes, but almost as prominently in the writings of Rousseau) are seen as prior to community in the viewpoint of all of these theorists. To Hobbes, solidarity in a community required only the realization that persons would be prevented from doing harm to each other; beneficence was not needed. Solidarity to Locke depended on mutual trust, and to Rousseau solidarity was a function of a social nexus resulting in the general will and actively promoting social good. Solidarity to Rousseau was endangered by modern, corrupted conditions gone astray.

One can, however, think of social contract in other ways.[19,20] Instead of seeing individuals as being necessarily prior to the formation of communities, which are formed only by contracting individuals, such a notion may be denied altogether. Rather, persons can be seen as being born into family and tribal groups and thus as emerging in communities. A social contract, in such a view, is a necessary part of any such group from the very start. Consistent with such an idea, contracts, rather than being formed in terror, are formed in the close embrace of a family, tribe, or like association. There is mutual bonding and the individual relies on the family or tribe for its nurture and sustenance. The tribe, in turn, needs individuals for its communal existence and requires its young for continuity. A much more complex and interactive model emerges, and such a model, rather than being based on terror, is based on bonds of mutual love, trust, needs and, inescapably, biosocial interdependence. As children grow up they may begin to fear others, and may, in fact, be in terror of those from other tribes or associations. But their initial social contract is a tacit one and is one made implicitly with those with whom they bond and who nurture and sustain them. Warmth, trust, and fellowship, therefore, are part of such an initial contract.

Families and tribes in turn may discover the need for a larger community and may then covenant with other tribes. Of course, the notion of mutual nonharm is critical: It is a necessary but far from sufficient condition for covenant. The very notion of covenanting and of nonharm must be seen as underwritten by trust if it is to come about in the first place or if it is to endure in the final analysis.[21] Without trust, people would be unlikely to emerge from behind their trees or rocks to covenant. Unless there is mutual trust, people cannot even think of covenanting together; unless there is mutual need (of which the need for protection from harm by others in the group is only a small part), no impulse for entering such associations exists. Trust, in turn, presupposes that, at the very least, our fellows care about our welfare and, where possible, are willing to come to our aid. A feeling of beneficence, then, is basic to such a theory.[20] Solidarity in such communities is not only a function of being left alone and not harmed, it is secured and cemented by reliance on mutual good will and beneficence. Modern societies could, if they did not surrender to crass individualism and greed, evolve without returning to an impossible-to-imagine "primitive" state.

In such a philosophy, the question of which came first, individuals or the communities of which they are a part, is a chicken-and-egg argument, both unanswerable and irrelevant. Social contract is an evolving entity. For the individual it starts in childhood with the family into which she is born. Gradually the community enlarges until individuals see themselves in the embrace of a complex set of communities. Like a Venn diagram, these communities overlap and create both the security of larger associations and the problems of reconciling differing world views. Individuals are suffused with communal values and shaped by communal customs. In truth, individuals cannot be imagined without communities into which they are born, in which they are reared and of which they remain a part. This is true even for those who withdraw from community for then the very act of withdrawal and the very notion of being withdrawn necessitate a prior concept of community. As, however, individual life experiences bring about changes in individuals, individuals in turn reshape communities. The evolution of the individual is as incomprehensible outside the community as the community is unimaginable without the individuals which compose it.[20]

The critical influence which viewpoints of social contract have on the way we envision community is obvious. When we feel obligated not to harm another even when we are most angry or, on the other hand, feel obliged to help another in need or distress, we base these feelings on a more general viewpoint of social contract. If we think that our initial coming together was grounded merely in mutual terror and that refraining from harming each other was sufficient condition for such a contract, we will see communities fashioned on a minimalist model which recognizes only obligations of mutual nonharm. On the other hand, if we see such a contract as not based on terror but assuming bonds of mutual love, trust, needs, and biosocial interdependence, a quite different viewpoint of community will emerge. The obligations we assume toward others in the community as well as toward the community itself, are directly linked to the way we see community being fashioned. Solidarity is what makes communities cohesive and solidarity is felt because the persons in community feel reasonably satisfied with their lot. The degree of satisfaction members feel is intimately linked with the solidarity their community develops.

Kant, the father of the modern concept of autonomy and the main figure we think of in that regard, saw the problem of beneficent duties clearly. He argues that negative or perfect duties are those absolutely incumbent on all persons at all times. Such duties, grounded in a respect for persons, are duties of logic. They accord with what he terms the "categorical imperative": categorical because it is binding at all times. Duties of nonharm, injunctions against lying, killing, or stealing are among these duties. But Kant saw beyond this. There are legitimate moral obligations of beneficence (not merely obligations for a particular moral enclave but moral obligations generally binding on all sentient beings). These are obligations not because one could not logically conceive of a world in which such duties did not exist but because to will otherwise would force the will to conflict with itself. All of us at some time or another in our lives are critically dependent upon the beneficent motives and actions of others.[2] Beneficent obligations, in Kant's view, are very much moral obligations but they are more optional: While we cannot, perhaps, always be beneficent we cannot, on the other hand, refrain from being beneficent altogether. The claim that Kant is the father of a minimalist ethic does not ring true.

I shall argue that the minimalist ethic (like that of Nozick and Engelhardt) is flawed in principle as well as in practice and that, therefore, beneficence inevitably enters the moral equation. Beyond this I shall advance the claim that autonomy necessarily develops in the embrace of beneficence and that autonomy initiates its necessary dialectic struggle with beneficence in the embrace of beneficence itself. I shall not only react to the autonomy based ethic and the minimalist community but give reasons why such a structure is unlikely as well as unworkable.

If we accept a Hobbesian view of social contract, a minimalist community emerges. Communities founded on a contract promising only mutual nonharm and nothing else are minimalist communities: communities in which freedom and autonomy are absolutes. Freedom and autonomy (as long as no explicit harm comes to one's fellow by the exercise of freedom and autonomy) are conditions and not values of the moral life. Respect for autonomy and protection of autonomy is what the ethical life is all about. Beneficence, caring, charity, all are nonmoral obligations. As envisioned by Nozick (and in the field of medical ethics by Engelhardt) obligations are of two sorts: (1) those of mutual nonharm (and, therefore, those respecting absolute freedom except as the exercise of such freedom would explicitly limit the autonomy of another); and (2) those freely assumed by explicit mutual contract. Beneficence is, perhaps, a most desirable sentiment but it carries no moral weight except as it may carry weight within particular moral enclaves. Such moral enclaves may freely exact beneficent obligations as a condition of membership internally, but their peculiar points of view have force only within the enclave itself. In a libertarian framework, it is difficult to see why beneficence is even a desirable sentiment. Beneficence no longer has moral weight but rather has an almost aesthetic value. Like raspberry sherbet or the music of Mozart, it may appeal to some but not to others. Its appeal is, from a moral point of view, idiosyncratic and purely volitional. Freely entered contracts in which both parties understand the terms must be allowed and strictly enforced no matter what their stipulations. According to libertarians, pluralist communities must constitute themselves in this fashion or remain forever in conflict. No moral point of view, except respecting the freedom of others, can be enforced upon all; all members are free to dissent and to go their own way except when it comes to directly injuring another or to violating freely entered, explicit, and mutually understood contracts.[22,23]

Communities structured in this fashion possess laws that limit private actions only insofar as such actions directly and immediately bring injury to a nonconsenting other. Even here, certain actions, such as dueling, though clearly injurious, might be allowable. Societies of this sort give entrepreneurism a free hand. Taxes can be imposed only insofar as the money is needed to insure the liberty of all citizens. It is the function of the state to maximize personal liberty for all limited only by everyone's obligation not to infringe the liberty of their fellows. Taxes to maintain police power sufficient to this end would be one of the few legitimate forms of taxation. Money from the wealthy for the benefit of the poor can be obtained only through voluntary contributions. The licensing of health professionals is not morally possible and drug or pure-food laws cannot be made or enforced. Physicians become "bureaucrats of health," vending machines who supply each patient with whatever he may want, regardless of the physician's own moral point of view and provided only that doing so is legal and that the patient promptly pays the stipulated sum. Solidarity (and, therefore, the peacefulness) of such communities emerges purely from the single obligation not to do each other harm. It is the necessary cement of such communities and, according to such a philosophy, it is also held to be sufficient.

When communities assume freedom as an absolute they are unable to balance freedom with other obligations and, therefore, they grow rigid. Such communities are often unable to evolve and grow. When communities of this sort are threatened by intolerable danger (say, an epidemic) and find that to counter the danger some restriction of personal liberties seems in order, they lack the necessary flexibility: They cannot exchange freedom for beneficence and cannot reach compromises. Dangers to the community cannot be reduced by compromising freedom in any way: Autonomy is absolute and cannot be attenuated. When inflexible communities finally violate their principles, as they are likely to do when an ongoing threat becomes overwhelming, such communities may well become much more oppressive than would flexible communities able to adapt themselves to changing circumstances. Tyranny can easily arrive in the Trojan horse of absolute freedom.[24,25]

It would be difficult, whether one followed a utilitarian model or a more deontologically oriented theory, to adopt a minimalist ethic. Autonomy as an absolute and the crass individualism which results from such a point of view do not easily lend themselves to producing the greatest good for the greatest number. Nor does a minimalist ethic care about that. For its purposes, it is sufficient only that no overt harm actively is done to any member of the community; facilitating the good (except as such a philosophy sees the general greatest good to flow from an absolute respect for autonomy) is not the issue. Utilitarians, in producing the greatest good for the greatest number, must, at least at times, be actively concerned with facilitating all their members good. Crass individualism and a minimalist ethic easily lend themselves to dominance of the weak and poor by the strong and rich.[26] Such a state of affairs is hardly likely to produce the greatest good for the greatest number, rather, it would produce the greatest good for the most capable and most powerful.

Deontologists, on the other hand, would be made uncomfortable by the insistence of the minimalist that beneficent obligations are not a moral matter. Kantian deontologists in particular would find that denying positive duties cannot be envisioned: To deny beneficent obligations would compel the will to conflict with itself.[2] Rule orientation could envision rules narrowly and solely focused on autonomy, but such an orientation would ultimately destroy rather than enhance an ethic principally focused on respect for persons as having moral worth in virtue of their capacity for autonomous choice. Respect denotes a measure of beneficence, an active interest in the welfare of others, and it logically demands not only that we refrain from actively harming those who are the objects of respect but likewise that we see to it that such people at the very least have their minimal needs met.

If, on the other hand, we follow a situational ethic (one where the maximalization of love, or agapism, is the underlying principle), an autonomy-based ethic most certainly will not do. This form of act-agapism is based on producing the most loving outcome, and, vague as that may be, it is hardly consistent with a cold philosophy which holds that beneficence is not a moral concern.[27,28] An ethic which endows entities that have the capacity to suffer with primary moral worth, likewise, cannot subscribe to a minimalist stance. While entities of primary worth who by definition have the capacity to suffer have a prima facie claim against having wanton suffering inflicted upon them,. far more than that is implied. Preventing suffering inevitably entails a due respect for beneficence: Relieving suffering is an obligation in such an ethic.[29]

Whatever theory one may wish to subscribe to, unless it is the Hobbesian theory of social contract and those of Nozick and Engelhardt which are parasitic upon it, one is compelled to acknowledge that beneficence forms an important part of the moral life. Indeed, even if one follows a Hobbesian notion, one could argue that autonomy and freedom cannot exist if, prior to their existence, the necessities of life are missing. To argue that autonomy and freedom cannot exist under conditions in which the necessities of life are missing will, however, be rejected by many minimalists. We cannot prevent others from having access to their basic needs but "having access" is defined by the minimalist purely in terms of not being actively prevented; facilitating access, seeing to it that access becomes a fact rather than merely a theoretical possibility, is not the issue for the hard-nosed minimalist.

The aim of any society is, first of all, to have peace. Without that, nothing else can be accomplished. Minimalists will argue that peace cannot be achieved unless autonomy is taken as the necessary and sufficient condition of a communal ethos. Unless autonomy is foremost, they argue, a pluralist society will inevitably be at war with itself. Only if all are left to do as they will, hedged in only by duties of mutual non-harm, can peace be assured. History, however, teaches otherwise. When the material needs of some members is not met while other members openly revel in their enjoyment of opulent luxuries, solidarity is shattered, peace vanishes, and, inevitably, revolution results. When the homeless are left to wander the streets, the hungry are left unfed, and the sick are without medical care, a situation practically inimical to peace results and only the brute force of a powerful state can prevent open warfare. But not forever.

The claim that a minimalist ethic based on an initial contract forged merely in terror is flawed in principle and flawed and reprehensible in practice can be shown to be true. In principle, as I have argued, the idea seems unlikely that any association or covenant could be founded merely on mutual terror and on nothing else. Sitting down at a table (or coming out from behind a rock or tree) in order to forge a covenant requires a far richer expectations than merely the avoidance of fear and terror. Not that fear of one another may not be a legitimate ingredient, but fear alone, while it may play a role in motivating us, does not supply a sufficient condition for us to leave the safety of our own lines. A belief—however minimal—that others can—however little—be trusted to keep an agreement is basic. Furthermore, there is no reason to believe that human beings raised in the embrace of a family would not have a good deal of trust towards their initial community, a feeling of trust inevitably necessary for widening the covenant. The impetus for widening such a covenant originates in a perception of mutual needs, love, and trust underwritten by an inevitable biosocial interdependence. To be established or maintained, solidarity grounded in satisfaction with the community necessitates more than an implied protection from a feared other. It is difficult to see, even in theory, how communities grounded merely in the alleviation of mutual terror could ever come about or how, in the final analysis, they could grow and sustain themselves.

In practice, communities of this sort have never existed and do not exist today. No nation, not even the most crassly capitalist, denies all obligations of beneficence. Nations tax the wealthy for the benefit of the poor even when they allow gaping loopholes and even when the benefit to the poor is grudging and grossly insufficient. At the very least, communities pay lip service to beneficent obligations. What is at issue in practice is not the moral status of beneficence but rather the extent to which beneficence should be a factor in moral equations. Allowing one's neighbor to starve while throwing away good food would seem, to most of us, to be reprehensible. Equally, societies which needlessly allow some to starve, freeze, or go without medical care while others live in opulence or squander enormous wealth does not accord with the vision of social justice most of us would lay claim to.

If we as individuals and communities have obligations, such obligations must be grounded in a basic assumption. It is my thesis that the basic assumptions, inseparable and inseparate, are a fundamental injunction against causing suffering and a belief that communal structure necessitates a commitment to beneficence. Whether one subscribes to an ontology which sees the communal ethos as emerging from a dialectic between individual and communal interests (as I do) or holds that respect for autonomy necessarily emerges from beneficence (as Pellegrino and Thomasma feel[30]) it is the extent and not the basic question of beneficent obligations which needs to be addressed.

No purely or largely reactive philosophy can be satisfying: We cannot simply react against a philosophy we do not like or think wrong without at least suggesting a positive view of our own to take its place. The philosophy of community I have begun to sketch has been largely reactive and it is woefully incomplete unless I at least also start to draw a positive point of view. This I am about to do.

Any philosophy of community structure must be grounded in a notion of social contract as well as in an idea of what gives objects moral standing.[28] Social contract is necessary to hold together any association, and an idea of what gives objects moral standing is crucial if obligation is to have any meaning. Such notions are not necessarily articulated but they nevertheless form the primordial grounding for community. Ultimately, articulating such ideas is a necessary part of examining communal structure. The idea of social contract implies obligations: obligations individuals have toward each other as well as obligations the members of a community have toward the community and, in turn, the legitimate expectations they may have of it.[29] In turn, the notion of obligation is incoherent without an understanding of why, and therefore to whom or to what, such obligations are owed. Social contract and some understanding of what gives entities moral worth are intimately linked.

I have previously suggested that to be owed a legitimate obligation implies a present or future capacity for suffering. We owe our obligations precisely because those affected by our actions would in some way be affected by them in a currently or potentially knowing way. When we feel obligations toward things which lack such a present or future capacity, we feel such obligations because acting toward such unknowing things would affect others who themselves are, in fact, knowing. Injuring material objects may be right or wrong depending on the effect our action has on another who actually or at least potentially knows. Symbolic objects (or ideas) have similar standing. This is not to imply that one can necessarily judge the merit of an action merely by its effect but it is to claim that whether it is the fact we intend or the effect we actualize, effect is inevitably part of the composite used to judge an act right or wrong.

Social contract implies a mutual assumption of obligations. As with most things such covenants have historical roots going into our murky primitive past as humans and, beyond this, our common past as knowing higher animals. To assume an arbitrary point at which such associations started and before which they did not exist is to break with the notion of evolution and, instead, to stake a claim in what almost amounts to creationism or spontaneous generation: a point at which something that was not is brought into being. Such a claim, when made

about any biological structure, would be widely acknowledged as ludi-
crous. Even when mutation occurs, it is a mutation which changes a
small aspect of a particular organism but still allows us to recognize not
only the new organism but also its antecedents.

Higher animals have certain implicit ways of association. Such
associations, or even the idea of association, is often stated to be a reflex:
a survival mechanism built into a species' genes. This sort of reflex
behavior, however, allegedly ends when man emerges. Man, it is
claimed, is a thinking animal, one whose decisions emanate from rational choice. Human beings, however, behave in accordance with their
biological framework no less than do gorillas or mountain goats. It is
just that the human framework is larger. Freedom of will operates
within a framework composed, in part, of our physical world and limited as well as partly programmed by our biological possibility.[1] Biological possibility, inevitably, includes the way our minds are structured.

When biological organisms form associations, they do so for reasons of survival. Social contract and its successful evolution is no less a
survival mechanism than, say, the development of a better sense of
smell. It helps individuals to survive but, more importantly in a biological sense, it helps ensure continuity and species survival. All things
being equal, species in which social contract works best, endure. Social
contract, in its initial inception, whether in its human or in its animal
form, is preknowing. Birds gather in flocks and wolves run in packs
because doing so is part of what it means to be a specific type of bird or
a wolf. Likewise, men associate in small, and ultimately, extended families called "tribes." Within this predetermined framework, the specifics
of pecking order or dominance remain to be worked out. Animals, like
humans, are born into such a contract, behave within its constraints,
and adapt it to their needs.

Humans differ from lower animals by virtue of having a history.
Human social contracts and the communities they spawn, therefore, are
not merely repetitive workings out of and adaptations to specific situations and changing physical forces but have continuity and the ability
to adapt over time. Individuals are born not only into a predetermined
biological framework but also into a historically evolved social context.
Both of these shape each person's perception, and, ultimately the way
individuals and communities act within their framework determines
the shape of the framework in the future.

From the most primitive time onwards, people have been born
into families. For that reason it seems unlikely that knowing associations evolved later than such primordial times. To claim that man was
first "solitary,"[16] entirely amoral albeit endowed with natural compas-

sion,[18] or able to have an economic system and a notion of property[17] before a contract ever came to pass is either to devise a definition of social contract to serve a purpose or to fly in the face of reason and experience.

Persons are necessarily born into families. Higher animals and humans cannot survive without parental support and nurture. Rousseau admits that this is the case but he holds that such associations are purely temporary. The way he sees it, when the young no longer require nurture such associations dissolve. While temporary ways of behaving toward one another in such associations have developed, morality has not been created and such early family associations still leave individuals amoral. This state comes to an end only when a knowing social contract is finally forged. The young, according to Rousseau, leave their families and enter the larger world as amoral beings.

When persons are born into families, nurtured by their parents and begin to mature, certain tacit assumptions exist. Infants, at first unable to differentiate self from nonself, develop their selfness in the embrace of a supportive and nurturing context. Even when the family is relatively cold, relatively uncaring, or when children are left to their own devices, a minimal amount of caring and nurture is necessary if individuals are not to perish. As individuals begin to become aware of the world outside themselves, as they differentiate self from nonself, they initially confront a benign world. Such a benign world encourages further exploration. The self differentiates in an initial context of caring and trust into which it can withdraw safely when, as must sooner or later happen, unpleasantness or danger are encountered. The world is not a benign place but it is explored from a vantage point in which beneficence is an implicit condition. Danger is encountered and met in this way. The necessity to explore underwrites the yearning for freedom and autonomy which all growing children experience. But the yearning for freedom and autonomy occurs in a context of preexistent beneficence.

Nurturing the young is undoubtedly a biologically programmed activity without which human survival would be impossible. Parents implicitly feel this obligation. Infants, in turn, develop their expectations of others from such a nurturing environment and assume obligations to others consistent with it. The infant shapes its view of mutual obligation from its experience of met and unmet expectations. It knows that suffering is to be avoided, it knows that, at the very least, a nurturing environment will minimize suffering, and, as a notion of selfhood develops, it assumes that other selves have developed in a similar way.

I have previously argued that compassion is a critical part of morality. Without such a sense, the recognition of what constitutes a moral problem (a problem which in some way involves our actions and their effect on others) is difficult if not impossible. Basing an ethic merely on logic begs the question of how we come to find out about moral problems in the first place. Without reflecting on our environment and on others', ethics is unthinkable. And our reflecting about and ultimately trying to understand and deal with others implies an ability to put ourselves in their place. It entails feeling for our fellows and, ultimately, compassion. Without such fellow feeling (without a sense of sharing the experience of other people), social contract, nurture, our sense of mutual obligation, and eventually community are unthinkable concepts. Even a legalistic formulation of ethical thought and a very legalistic formulation of obligation must rest on a recognition of others and upon a sense of compassion.

A sense of obligation can only come about when infants learn that the world and they are not identical and when they have undergone the process of differentiating self from nonself. Before other selves are recognized, obligations or a sense of obligation cannot exist. As this evolution takes place, it is critically dependent upon the nurture of others. A sense of self inevitably develops in the embrace of a nurturing environment. An environment which totally fails to nurture such a completely dependent being is not an environment in which such a being can survive. As infants develop a sense of self, their fledgling autonomy is forged in the context of beneficence and is ensured by their community. Fear of others, resentment of others in competing for the space an emerging autonomy requires, develops and is shaped by the largely beneficent expectations of others which the child experienced and came to rely upon early in life. Beneficence and the beneficent community are ontologically prior to fear, jealousy, and the struggle to achieve personal autonomy. The feeling of what is owed to others and what others owe one is inevitably conditioned by that history.

Beneficence (doing good to others) and its caricature, paternalism (imposing one's own vision of what is good on others quite regardless of their wishes), vie with a developing autonomy. Beneficence, by focusing on doing good to others in general, involves a sense of community; beneficence that is only personally directed, which seeks to do good only to specific others, is merely an expression of a wider personal autonomy in which the beneficent act is still done merely to conform to personal whim. Autonomy focuses on the individual self. It is the ultimate step in differentiating self from all else, emancipating it and, finally, denying all else except as it may threaten one's own personal existence. The forces promoting beneficence and those promoting autonomy keep each other in check.

Beneficence and autonomy vie with each other in an ongoing dialectic from which one's world view emerges. This is as true for communities, whose sense of obligation and whose ethos results from such a dialectic, as it is for the individual. Inevitably since the ongoing dialectic takes place in the context of social contract and implicit obligation, these forces shape the form of the dialectic and, in turn, are shaped by it. Social contract is an evolving vision, a vision with ancient historical roots, a current expression and a future to be developed. It is not an unchanging, mute form to which the present as well as the future must accommodate itself.

If one views autonomy as emerging from beneficence, as Pellegrino and Thomasma do, the same tensions remain.[30] Beneficence, if it is to be truly beneficent, can neither simply unleash autonomy nor can it entirely stifle it by keeping it on too short a leash. Autonomy must and will have to have its say but it must have it within a framework of beneficence. Once the individual's desire for autonomy emerges, it inevitably will struggle with the forces—beneficent or otherwise—seeking to restrain it. Out of this tension a framework of action emerges within which persons are free to seek their own destiny. Unless perverted, this framework will be a nurturing one. Parents ultimately seek to foster their children's autonomy in the same way and for much the same reason that larger communities seek to foster the autonomy of their members: Just as survival of the young child is critically dependent on beneficent nurture, optimal function and survival later in life depend upon establishing an adult autonomy ready to stand on its own feet but mindful of its communal roots and obligations.

Social contract has its roots in the family. In turn, families cannot exist completely alone. Human biology and the study of anthropology suggest that the most primitive peoples lived in extended families and tribes. Such associations require unspoken assumptions, tacit agreements, and social givens. Without such implicit understandings associations cannot endure. Individuals within such associations rely on mutual help even when they are at war with other tribes. There are, of course, limits to mutual help. At times some individuals, injured, old, or otherwise burdensome to the community must be abandoned. Such abandoning, however, is part of a social contract rooted in nurture but firmly committed to communal survival.

Persons value their freedom and treasure their autonomy. Such yearnings, however, imply a community in which freedom and autonomy can express themselves and play themselves out. Speaking of freedom and autonomy outside a context of community is incoherent. What freedom and autonomy of entirely solitary creatures might be cannot even be envisioned. A concept of being free to act (within biological and physical constraints) outside a community with none to hinder such action would be an implicit condition of such a life. Freedom to act, to be meaningful, requires other actors just as a beam of light requires relative darkness to be perceived. Even if, which seems unlikely, a totally solitary state could endure, it can be such a state only after the necessary dependence of youth is over. Furthermore, since man is basically a social animal, such a solitary state would be meaningless, empty, and, inevitably, without progeny and thus short-lived.

Persons have obligations not only to themselves and to their contemporaries but to the future of others like them. This claim rests, among other things, on the fact that we have a history: a history which includes the concern of those who came before us for our existence today. The fact that we have survived inevitably demonstrates that we have been the recipients of individual nurture and concern, a nurture and concern without which we ourselves could not be. Future generations are not absent today and suddenly present tomorrow. The borders between the past, the present, and the future are blurred and cannot be strictly delineated; rather, the past, and the future are joined in a continuum that extends forward and back far beyond vision. Mutuality of obligation, likewise, is a continual process and not one which has definite, clearly defined, or clearly definable temporal borders. We have obligations to tomorrow because we and others like us had a yesterday to which we are inevitably linked and because we cannot in a communal rather than a merely personal sense delineate the past, the future, and the present. Our own past, our own present, and our own future may be delineable: We were born at a given time and will, at some specific moment, cease to exist. Obligations owed us specifically start and stop at definable points. Communities, however, provide the necessary stability within which such delineations can occur. For this reason communities cannot themselves be that easily delineated: They extend over time and merge the past with the future as the actors slowly appear, disappear, and overlap.[31]

Communities, although composed of individuals, predate their members. Since lower animals lack the ability to transmit and develop their communal history, communities of animals largely have a nonevolving social contract. (There has been occasional evidence, however, especially in primates, that this is not entirely true.) They repeat their basic communal history changed only because of environmental changes in forces outside their community and beyond their control. Some features of human social contract, likewise are evidently unchanging. People are born into and nurtured by families (or, if not by families, still nurtured by an essentially safe environment) and develop a basic sense of mutual obligation in the embrace of such a family or group. Further, their own experience counsels them to avoid suffering, and reason implicitly recommends that their own experience is equally applicable to others. A sense of obligation unavoidably is nourished by these roots.

Communities are composed of individuals themselves the product of community and equipped with a sense of obligation. Life experiences mold individuals and inevitably this forces visions of social contract, obligation, and, ultimately, community to evolve. It is the structure of community that is based on a vision of social contract, which is in turn grounded in family and allowing the evolution of selves, to which I now turn.

If one accepts that communities are based on implicit social contract and believes that individual selves came to develop their sense of obligation out of the experience of early nurture as well as out of their avoidance of suffering, and furthermore if one believes that such an initial vision of contract and obligation is further molded by social forces, a complex and ever-changing model of community emerges. Common needs give the impulse to form associations. Associations, to sustain themselves, must continue to have common needs as well as having trust in each other. Without original need, no impulse to form associations exists, without continued mutual need and without trust in each other no enduring association is possible. The family remains a unit largely because its members care for each other's welfare and because they translate such caring into benevolent intention and beneficent action. Children, as they become full-fledged members of specific communities, carry with them the knowledge of early nurture and the reliance on benevolence which such nurture entails.

In the distant past, wider communities slowly coalesce responsive to common needs and to the changing material circumstances which the early development of primitive civilizations entailed. Changing material circumstances created changing needs and made the formation of larger and more complex associations advisable. Changing material circumstances, however, helped forge new contracts from the old; they were the setting for a changing adaptive contract but did not bring about an initial social contract. The formation of such communities, just as the formation of previous smaller associations, still occurred in a context of beneficence and mutual trust. Indeed, while fear (especially the fear of external threats) was a motivating factor, caring, trust, and an interest in each other's welfare were as necessary as ever to allow formation and continuity. The basic obligation of respect for others capable of suffering as we were ourselves capable of suffering, trust that others were involved in our weal and woe and ongoing mutual needs, were at least as important as was fear.

Communities as they exist today can be seen as fashioned from such a view of social contract. If one adopts a view of social contract which denies the ontological priority of individuals (or which simply shrugs off the question as unanswerable and irrelevant) and sees social contract as an evolving one necessitated by mutual needs, love, trust, and biosocial interdependence, an initial contract necessitating beneficence clearly emerges. Such communities will not make freedom—or anything else—an absolute condition but, rather, will be able to adjust their values and formulate their policies in a dynamic fashion. When freedom is not an absolute condition of the moral life but rather one of its esteemed values, a dialectic between individual autonomy and communal needs emerges. Such a dialectic is similar to an Aristotelian striving for the mean. Beneficence, in such a community, may well be held to be a condition prior to respecting autonomy: One cannot, as Pellegrino and Thomasma have so clearly pointed out, be truly beneficent to anyone without having a high regard for that person's wishes and points of view.[30] A respect for autonomy clearly emerges from a beneficence-based ethic; the obverse—that a regard for beneficence necessarily emerges from an autonomy-based ethic—is clearly not the case.

Communities built on a beneficent model are communities in which laws could limit private actions when such limitations clearly benefit the values held by the community. Clearly injurious actions, such as dueling, can be proscribed if a sufficient number of the members of the community feel such an action to be inconsistent with its ideals. Societies of this sort are apt to limit crass entrepreneurism when it is seen to interfere with the community's welfare. Taxes can be imposed on all citizens, if imposing such taxes is seen as necessary for promoting the welfare of all members. Taxing the wealthy for the benefit of the truly poor, and guaranteeing minimal subsistence to all members, is apt to become the order of the day. Health professionals can be licensed and drug or pure-food laws and other laws to promote the welfare and safety of the citizenry can be made and enforced. Physicians now are more than merely "bureaucrats of health." No longer are they seen and see themselves merely as vending machines who supply patients with whatever patients may want regardless of the physician's own moral point of view. Their own moral viewpoints matter and while they are not entitled to force their viewpoint down the patient's throat neither are they obligated to provide services they themselves may feel are professionally uncalled for or, in their own view, feel to be immoral. The relationship of health professionals to their charges now is one of mutual trust, beneficence has a legitimate, and perhaps a central, moral role. The solidarity (and, therefore, the peacefulness) of such communities can be seen to emerge from an interplay of forces based on an initial social contract firmly grounded in mutual needs, love, trust, and biosocial interdependence. Beneficence, as well as the respect for autonomy which must go with it, is the necessary cement of such communities and, according to this philosophy, beneficence and all that flows from it is held to be a necessary condition of the moral life.

When communities balance and reassess their values in an ongoing fashion, they maintain flexibility. Such communities can evolve and grow. As circumstances change, such communities will feel that they can adapt their particular behavior to current needs. Not free to savage their member's autonomy at will, they can, nevertheless, not overlook the welfare of all. When such communities confront a threat to the public good (say, are confronted with the threat of an epidemic) they can make compromises and work out accommodations in a timely fashion. Since such compromises and accommodations do not violate but indeed are consistent with the underlying principles of association, these compromises and accommodations are far less likely to result in tyranny and oppression.

Specific communities and specific individuals form their particular moral world-view out of the tension of communal and individual interests. Individual morality is shaped by the tension which exists when we must balance our own narrow interest with the interest of another or of others. If we feel that we owe largely or solely duties of nonharm, our basic ethos will be quite different than if we feel strongly about accepting beneficent obligations. The difference between altruist and egoist is shaped from such material. Communal morality, likewise, is shaped by these forces. The tension between the requirements of individual liberty and the demands of social justice exemplifies this.

Communities and individuals rarely are either entirely individualistic or entirely beneficent. When individuals are entirely unmindful of their beneficent obligations, we speak of them as crass egoists (the psychopath goes a step further: She fails to accept even obligations of nonharm); when communities fail entirely to acknowledge beneficence, they cease being communities and shatter. Not even the crassest capitalist state is entirely without;some redeeming beneficence. The Ikhs, of which Engelhardt speaks[23] (a group of disadvantaged, poverty-stricken natives clinging to a barren mountainside and allegedly without an impulse to beneficence), are not an example of a community in which beneficence has no role but of a community in which solidarity has been shattered and which, consequently, has failed. Entirely beneficent individuals, abrogating every shred of self-interest are dangerous saints who may readily sacrifice their neighbor for what they perceive to be that neighbor's good. Communities in which beneficence reigns supreme, likewise are apt to see beneficence as enforcing and regimenting their own peculiar vision of the good. Such communities will readily sacrifice their members for the sake of their own ideology.

The problem, on an individual or communal basis, is not with extremes. In truth, the absolute extreme cannot exist or, when it exists, it is self-destroying. The problem is that all too often the synthesis emerging from the dialectic of communal and individual interests seems very far from a rational mean and leads to unnecessary and often sustained suffering. I want to turn to an examination of this problem.

Respect for individual rights (or as we in the West are apt to call it, "human rights," as though the fulfillment of basic human needs were not a human right!) is what makes individual fulfillment and flourishing possible. Individual rights, however, are necessarily a later concern than social justice. Social justice (as though respecting individual rights were not a necessary part of meaningful social justice!), however, enables the minimal conditions for biological and social existence. Much as life can be viewed as the necessary condition for experience (experience without life is not possible), so social justice can be seen as necessary for the existence of individual rights. Persons who are hungry, cold, homeless, ignorant, or ill, will find little comfort in the realization that they may freely assemble or speak. Persons who have their basic needs met but the opportunity for personal expression and flourishing denied, will find little joy in what has now become mere existence. The hungry, cold, homeless, ignorant, or ill suffer equally with those denied a reasonable freedom to express their unique personality and to flourish.

When communities are structured in a truly democratic fashion by an informed, educated, interested, aware, and caring electorate, the dialectic between the demands of the community and the requirements of personal liberty tends to prevent extreme swings. The problem comes about either when choices given to the electorate are limited by powerful forces or when the electorate either lacks free expression, is theoretically able to express itself but lacks awareness of the facts or the necessary education to bring the facts into proper perspective, or when it has become indolent, apathetic, and noncaring.

When beneficence becomes extreme it can easily be perverted into paternalism. On an individual basis this results in those who deal from positions of power defining what is good for others and then forcing their vision on their charges who have now become victims. Medicine and the all-too-frequently paternal practice of medicine provides an excellent example. In such circumstances, patients are voiceless and no longer able to control their own destiny. On a communal level, when beneficence becomes extreme and perverted, the state decides what is good for its now disenfranchised members and enforces its will.

When the balance tilts too much toward autonomy, persons are apt to be abandoned to their autonomy. Again medicine and medical practice can give examples. Panicky, poorly informed or confused patients whose autonomy is at the very least severely limited can be abandoned to such a strange definition of "autonomy." A community valuing autonomy too highly is apt to have a strange view of social justice. Unrelieved or minimally and grudgingly relieved poverty, homelessness, hunger, ignorance, and illness are apt to proliferate. The excuse that the poor, hungry, homeless, and ignorant have chosen this state for themselves, or that they had as much opportunity as anyone else and merely failed to seize it, are not infrequently offered as excuses for such a state of affairs. Undue respect for autonomy gives a convenient and growing edge to the powerful and allows them to perpetuate their power.

The powerless, poor, and ignorant lack the means for controlling their own destiny and often lack even hope; disaffection and unhappiness have produced apathy. When higher education is available only at great financial sacrifice and when it is, therefore, often unavailable to those who are poor or even often to those of moderate income, another opportunity to gain access to power is foreclosed. When the powerful have much to say about basic education and when the powerful control the media, facts tend to be distorted and the ability to examine available facts becomes attenuated. What results is a powerful capitalist state with the capacity and the will to directly and indirectly control so-called free elections and to shape public opinion or to keep it apathetic. Such states, when they go too far, may lack the ability to right themselves.

Speaking of "community" remains unclear unless what is meant is carefully spelled out. I have claimed that community originates in the family and in the nurture experienced by infants as they develop their sense of self and begin to stretch their fledgling autonomy in the embrace of similarly beneficent communities. Such communities relate to and with other similar communities, and inevitably mingle. When I speak of community, I do not have a static entity in mind but rather see community as a fluid association and relationship. Starting with the family and the extended family and progressing outward, communities extend and interlock until they encompass the world.

As infants reflect on their environment and on their relationships with others, they necessarily develop compassion and fellow feeling: One cannot successfully reflect about others without trying to put one-self in their shoes. Beneficence and compassion ultimately underpin the implicit social contract and, through it, community. Beneficent communities, as I have tried to show, do not exist in a vacuum. Communities are themselves embedded in larger communities with which they relate and in which they share as members. Such relationships and such sharing necessitates communal reflection on more than merely itself. Humans as sentient and social animals reflect on their environment and on their relationships, a process which I have advanced the claim necessarily entails some fellow feeling and compassion. A smaller community and its members, therefore, cannot entirely disregard the welfare of the communities with which it interrelates. In a real sense we are they and they are us. In today's world, such relationships are universal. To claim that what happens in Kuwait, Sri Lanka, or Uganda does not really concern us and to claim, as a corollary, that we have no responsibility for the welfare of others in such distant communities is not a credible, even if often heard, claim. The individualism of communities (the claim that we do not have to concern ourselves with other communities except as such concern directly affects our narrow self-interest) is inimical to solidarity just as the individualism of individuals within a community is. A world which fails to accept this will be a world without solidarity and, eventually, without more than a tenuous peace based merely on mutual terror.

Whenever the concept of community is raised, those raising it are accused of a certain form of vagueness: Just what is meant by the term "community," and what are the relationships involved—not only between individuals and the community of which they are a part but among various communities? In today's world we want every *i* dotted and every *t* crossed, insist on explicit answers to every question, and want technically perfect models. We are uncomfortable with the whole notion of evolution and growth in which answers are always tentative and in which solutions do not come in neat and final packages. The whole notion of inquiry as an ongoing process which merely makes indeterminacy less indeterminate is not a popular one. Rather, we would like to look at inquiry as able to provide a final solution to our problems.[32] Expecting such final solutions, expecting all *i*'s to be dotted and all *t*'s to be crossed, is an obviously unfulfillable expectation and one which flies in the face of historical evidence. Historically speaking, yesterday's solutions merely become tools with which to unravel tomorrow's problems. Hoping for solutions or expecting explanations to be anything more than tentative or to do anything other than give a solution that is somewhat better than the one we had yesterday but still far from perfect is historically unrealistic, fundamentally arrogant, and, basically, immature.

The problems of exactly defining communities and delineating the exact relationships between community and the individuals or smaller communities which compose it is, likewise, an evolutionary process. Communities are more than merely associations of people.[33] Mere associations of people can be formed by individuals who share merely congruent interests and who see such interests as individual and potentially opposed. Such an association is then seen as only a means towards private and individual ends.

Real communities consist of more than a sharing of individual interests which, by chance, happen to coincide. True communities see in their association far more than merely a means to an individually perceived and defined good. The association itself is seen as one of the goods. In a mere association, individuals who have used the association as a means toward attaining a private good will stand ready to abandon the association once the goal is attained. It has served its purpose. Members of a true community share values and goals which become communal values and goals rather than remaining merely private interests which at a given time happen to coincide.[34] Beyond this, however, an association which has become a community is seen as a good, a goal and a value having its own standing. The community's gain is perceived as a personal gain, a gain not separable into individual component parts. When pursuing common values and goals members consider themselves as members of the group rather than as isolated individuals. While such an attitude lessens an individual's perception of what is his private property or interest and subsumes such interest into that of the community, it does not follow that all interests or property share in this. Rather common values and goals are such in part because accepting them permits more effective individual flowering. Private flowering occurs within the context of community and is seen as enhancing rather than diminishing community. Without individual growth opening the door to new ideas and new activities, communities would not, or at least would not as easily, evolve and themselves flourish and grow.

A community then is seen as an evolving entity, underwritten by a social contract conceived in the necessary nurture and beneficence shown toward the infant whose differentiation of self from nonself occurred in that setting and whose fledgling autonomy, therefore, began in the context of beneficence. A community is constituted not only to prevent mutual harm but, where possible, to ameliorate suffering. Solidarity in such a community is seen as cemented by the realization that all are concerned in each other's welfare and will, to the extent possible, focus their resources on furthering this shared value. The relationship of the individuals to community is one of mutual necessity: Individuals need community to express, to enunciate, and to enable their personal flowering and communities need individuals to continue their own communal existence and growth.

Such a conception may underwrite specific communities but does little to enable the living together of disparate communities so necessary in our even smaller and yet pluralist world. People have assumed that such communities would still find little to unite them with other communities and that, therefore, inevitable strife would result. The problem with such a point of view, I think, is the assumption that small communities are much the way that libertarians conceive individuals to be: solitary, nasty, and brutish with a stake only in mutual nonharm and no possible common stake in values beyond this. They are seen as quite separate and separable entities whose relationship to the greater community in which they are inevitably imbedded is most problematic. The only solution to such a quandary is the libertarian one of either making of freedom and autonomy an absolute or, at least, making of it a value so high that few other points of contact remain. Such an assumption falls into the basic libertarian error of starting with individuals covenanting to form associations rather than looking at associations as individuals necessarily united by common values and goals. Individual communities no more developed in a solitary, nasty, and brutish state of nature than did individuals themselves. Communities share implicit goals, goals which unite all people and, indeed, which unite all sentient beings into a common family. The avoidance and, where possible, amelioration of suffering forms such an implicit basis and necessitates far more than merely a decent respect for autonomy; it requires the cement of beneficence if solidarity is to occur and strife is to be avoided.

Larger communities relate to smaller ones in the same organic way in which small communities relate to the individuals of which they are composed. Their ontology is similar and basically starts with the nurture necessarily part of an individual's early experience as well as with the common denominator of preventing or ameliorating suffering. Just as individuals in Rousseau's supposed state of nature were endowed with a primitive sense of pity, communities are endowed

with a sense of curiosity and concern which eventuates in a caring attitude towards each other. As they develop, communities—just like individuals—necessarily reflect on themselves and on each other. Far from
being born hating and fearing, they must be taught to hate and fear and
such teaching, if indeed it takes place, occurs in the preceding embrace
of curiosity, caring, nurture, and beneficence.

Rousseau's "general will," the fundamental expression of the
goals and values uniting individual communities, likewise has a larger
expression in the general will emanating from a larger community and
ultimately the human family. The shared values and goals of such a
community can start with the unifying value inherent in avoiding and,
where possible, ameliorating the suffering of all its members, whether
they are individuals composing a small community or communities
composing a larger family. Just like a community whose solidarity
depends on far more than merely mutual nonharm, a united world will
not remain long united when mutual nonaggression rather than mutual
help is the only force prompting solidarity.

When smaller communities are formed in an individualistic manner, that is, in a way in which they see themselves as solitary individual
communities outside the context of the larger world, they readily
embrace a form of strident nationalism. Such communities see themselves as facing other communities with whom they must alternately
compete and cooperate to further their own good rather than to strive
towards a common goal. Often, and then to safeguard their own interests and to more effectively pursue their own goals, they will enter
nonaggression pacts or perhaps even forge temporary alliances with
others, but they do so because they share congruent and usually temporary interests. At other times they see their interests as being individual
and potentially opposed. The association of such communities is seen
merely as a means toward their particular community's private and
individual ends.

Larger human communities, and ultimately the world community, properly consist of smaller communities sharing far more than
merely temporary individual interests which, by chance, happen to
coincide. Their association does not merely serve as a means toward
ends defined by individual communities for themselves. The world
community itself is seen as one of the shared goods. When communities
see themselves as being part of an association merely to promote their
own individual values and goals, they will stand ready to abandon the
association once the goal is attained. Members of a world community
must see themselves as sharing values and goals which become everyone's and every community's values and goals rather than remaining

merely private interests which at a given time happen to coincide. A gain for any one community is, ultimately, seen as a gain for all and as a gain for the very idea of community itself. The nationalistic striving for one community's success at the expense of another is seen as a Pyrrhic victory since it entails diminishing community and, ultimately, defeats the very success it has tried to bring about. While such an attitude lessens the striving for narrow national success and subsumes such a national interest into that of the community, it does not follow that all interests necessarily share in this. The common values and goals themselves underwrite a more effective flowering on the part of individual communities, allowing them to express and develop their own traditions and cultures most effectively. The larger association itself has become a good, a goal, and a value shared by the various component communities. Development of individual traditions and cultures occurs within the context of a larger family and is seen as enhancing, rather than reducing, the family itself. Developing individual traditions and cultures opens the door to new ideas and new activities allowing the family itself to evolve and grow.

The community, then, as we have sketched it is a dynamic association. Communities and their members, in the narrow and in the wider sense of community, interact with each other to solve ongoing problems and by so doing allow community to flourish and evolve. Based on respect and compassion for the individual's real or potential suffering as well as created in a basic atmosphere of nurture, communities must chart their own destiny. When the dialectic between beneficent communal obligations and a proper desire for personal autonomy is adjudicated in an ongoing process in which all knowingly and compassionately participate, an acceptable balance can be achieved.

To feel comfortable in a community and to feel a sense of solidarity with it and with one's neighbor implies more than an assurance that one's neighbor will not actively hurt one. Such security, of course, is essential. But we can be quite sure that distant people will not actively hurt us without feeling solidarity with them. Solidarity requires more secure footing. To feel comfortable within a community and to feel a sense of solidarity with one's neighbors also implies that we and our neighbors are connected by a thread of caring for each other's good, that we are ready to provide some nurture and some sense of beneficence for and to each other. When a sense of compassion and beneficence is not a part of community, community will lose cohesiveness and shatter. When the balance swings so far toward autonomy that a few individuals or nations enjoy sumptuous luxuries while many others go without having basic needs met, solidarity becomes difficult to maintain and the pressure for change, and eventually for violent change, mounts. As such pressure mounts it can be relieved by wise, timely, and compassionate measures which necessarily will take resources from those who have the most for the benefit of those who are in want. Solidarity may then be maintained and preserved. If, on the other hand, repressive measures are employed to safeguard individual liberty and property, rather than making compromises and limiting some freedoms to insure sufficient resources for all, the pressure will mount until an inevitable explosion occurs. Once solidarity has disappeared or become minimal, community cannot be long maintained.

Communities which have achieved an acceptable balance will inevitably care for their members weal and woe. Justice in such communities at the very least will try its best to provide all members with basic needs even when doing so may deprive some others of excess material goods. Ameliorating the unnecessary suffering of some members will take priority over allowing others a sumptuous and opulent lifestyle. This is as true within smaller communities as it is for the wider communal relationship. Such a point of view will be acceptable to most who recognize and accept beneficent obligations, who feel obligated to prevent suffering and who subscribe to a social contract emerging from beneficence. Differences will arise when what is and what is not acknowledged to be a "need" is unclear and conflict can only be resolved by providing clear definitions of needs. It is to this that I will turn in the next chapter.

## References

1. Dennet DC: *Elbow Room: The Varieties of Free Will Worth Having*. Cambridge: MIT Press, 1985.

2. Kant I: *Grundlegung zur Metaphysik der Sitten*. E. Cassirer and A. Buchenau, eds. Berlin: Bruno Cassirer, 1918.

3. Sophocles: *Antigone*. E. Wyckoff trans. In: *Greek Tragedies*. D. Green, R. Lattimore, eds. Chicago: University of Chicago Press, 1960.

4. Homer: *Odyssey* A. Cook, trans. New York: W. W. Norton & Co., 1967.

5. Plato: Laws. A. E. Taylor trans. In: *Plato, the Collected Dialogues*. E. Hamilton and C. Huntington eds. Princeton, NJ: Princeton University Press, 1961.

6. Aristotle: *Nichomachean Ethics*. M. Ostwald trans. Indianapolis: Bobbs-Merrill Publishers, 1962.

7. Copleston FC: *Aquinas*. New York: Penguin Books, 1988.

84 *Suffering and the Beneficent Community*

8. Mill JS: *Utilitarianism*. Indianapolis: Hackett Publishers, 1979.

9. Prichard HA: *Moral Obligation*. Oxford: Clarendon Press, 1968.

10. Dewey J: *Outlines of a Critical Theory of Ethics*. New York: Greenwood Press, 1957.

11. Dewey J: *Theory of the Moral Life*. New York: Irvington Publishers, 1980.

12. Gough W: *The Social Contract*. New York: Oxford University Press, 1957.

13. Laslett P: Social Contract. In: *The Encyclopedia of Philosophy*. P. Edwards, ed. New York: Macmillan, 1972.

14. Levin M: Social Contract. In: *Dictionary of the History of Ideas*. P. P. Wiener, ed. New York: Macmillan, 1972.

15. Loewy EH: *A Textbook of Medical Ethics*. New York: Plenum Publishers, 1989.

16. Hobbes T: *Leviathan*. New York: Collier, 1962.

17. Locke J: *Second Treatise of Government*. C. E. Macpherson, ed. Indianapolis: Hackett Publishing, 1980.

18. Rousseau JJ: *Du Contrat Social*. R. Grimsley, ed. Oxford: Oxford University Press, 1972.

19. Loewy EH: Communities, Entrepreneurialism and Health Care. In: *The Clinical Relationship: Towards a Hermenutical Perspective*. D. Schultz and G. Sherlock, eds. Indianapolis: University of Indiana Press, 1989.

20. Loewy EH: Commodities, Needs and Health Care: A Community Perspective. In: *Changing Values in Medicine and Health Care Decision Making*. V. J. Jensen and G. Mooney, eds. London: Wiley Publishers, 1990.

21. Loewy EH: Communities, Self-Causation and the Natural Lottery. *Soc Sci Med* 26:1133-39, 1988.

22. Nozick R: *Anarchy, State and Utopia*. New York: Basic BOoks, 1974.

23. Engelhardt HT: *The Foundations of Bioethics*. New York: Oxford University Press, 1986.

24. Loewy EH: Not by Reason Alone: A Review of H. Tristram Engelhardt's *Foundations of Bioethics*. *J Med Humanities and Bioeth* 8(1):67-72, 1987.

25. Loewy EH: AIDS and the Human Community. *Soc Sci Med* 27(4):297-303, 1988.

26. Niebuhr R: Rationing and Democracy. In: *Love and Justice*. D. R. Robertson, ed. Philadelphia: Westminster Press, 1957.

27. Fletcher J: *Situation Ethics*. Philadelphia: Westminster Press, 1966.

28. Loewy EH: Suffering, Moral Worth and Medical Ethics: A New Beginning. *Bridges* 1(3/4):107-41, 1989.

29. Loewy EH: "Social Contract, Communities and Guardians" *Journal of Elder Abuse and Neglect* 1990 (in publication).

30. Pellegrino ED and Thomasma DC: *For the Patient's Good: The Restoration of Beneficence to Health Care.* New York: Oxford University Press, 1988.

31. Loewy EH: AIDS: Ethical and Communal Issues in AIDS: An Introduction. *Theoretical Medicine* 11:173-183, 1990.

32. Dewey J: *Logic, the Theory of Inquiry.* New York: Henry Holt & Co., 1938.

33. Postema G: Collective Evil, Harms and the Law: Review of *The Moral Limits of the Criminal Law,* vols. 1 and 2 by J. Feinberg. *Ethics* 997:418-23, 1987.

34. Buchanan AE: Assessing the Communitarian Critique of Liberalism. *Ethics* 99:852-82, 1989.

# Chapter Five

# The Nature of Needs

If we are to agree that communities have obligations of beneficence as well as having obligations to respect individual autonomy, we
inevitably will come face to face with the notion of needs. Communities
which acknowledge duties of beneficence will, at the very least, be concerned with facilitating access to what they conceive to be the critical
needs of their members. Minimalist communities in which beneficence
has no moral standing, on the other hand, may acknowledge that certain things are needs (and, indeed that they are critical needs) but will
envision the community's obligations merely as making sure that no
one's access to such needs is prevented by another. Both types of communities will need to define needs, but defining what is or is not a need
and contrasting such a notion to one of a want will have far more practical consequences in a beneficent than it will in a minimalist community.

Beyond this, when the dialectic between communal (beneficent)
obligations and individual autonomy swings heavily towards autonomy (when, in other words a very high value is attached to individual
liberties and only a very small value to beneficence) the concept of
needs will tend to be much more rigorously defined than it would be in
a community in which beneficent obligations have a higher value. Not
only the perception of the obligation to meet needs but the very way in
which needs are defined varies with our notion of social contract and
our consequent vision of communal structure and obligation. People
more concerned with their neighbors' flourishing will tend to envision
their neighbors' needs far more broadly and far more generously than
will those indifferent to their neighbors' fortunes and concerned only
with their own individual fates.

What is and what is not a need, in the model I am developing, is grounded in a notion of suffering. Individuals have a prima facie obligation not to cause suffering and wherever possible to ameliorate it; communities are cemented by far more than the mutual agreement among its members to leave each other alone. Solidarity in communities, the way I have sketched it, is critically dependent on the realization of its members that they are free to pursue their private interests but equally that they are members of an association which deeply and genuinely cares about its members wellbeing. Communities are not only means to the fulfillment of individual goals, they underwrite the possibility of such goals. When solidarity is established, community itself becomes a goal of association.[1,2]

This chapter is concerned with basic needs and with their distribution. *Basic needs* will mean one of two things: (1) *basic need* may mean a "first-order necessity": something required to sustain primitive biological existence and its goals. Air, food, warmth, and shelter are examples; or (2) *basic need* may mean a certain kind of "second-order necessity": something required to sustain acceptable existence within a given social context so that reasonable individual goals can be met. Health care and education are examples. *Basic* here is intended to denote something of fundamental importance, something which serves to support the form of life as well as allowing a socially determined sufficient content.

In the state of nature (Engelhardt's by now famous Ba Mbuti are an example[3]), first-order necessities are the crux of the matter and second-order necessities, taken for granted in the modern, industrialized world, are either unknown and unimaginable or of little use in realizing reasonable individual goals. Other, socially structured second-order necessities, perhaps incomprehensible to us, take their place. All biological beings have critical needs: things needed to sustain existence itself. All biological beings within communities also will have other needs, needs which are needs because they are necessary to sustain acceptable existenced within the particular social context of a particular community. In modern industrialized societies (hardly in a state of nature) first-order necessities, or the second-order necessities of primitive tribes, cannot suffice to permit a realization of reasonable individual goals. Those things we recognize as second-order necessities, although far different from those in primitive societies, become essential if such goals are to be met.

There are, of course, needs which are seen as needs merely by a given individual or group of individuals. The goals which such needs serve, however, are goals which individuals define for themselves commensurate with their peculiar tastes. I may feel a compelling need to go to concerts or to travel abroad, but fulfilling such a need neither serves to underwrite my biological existence nor allows me access to a full and reasonable opportunity range in the context of our particular society. I shall call such needs third-order necessities and shall maintain that it is such needs that usually are what we term "wants."

One cannot discuss the concept of needs within the context of any particular segment of the community (say, what constitutes a need in health care) without first thoroughly examining the general concept itself. Needs must be distinguished from mere wants. The one is important and has a far higher and perhaps even a different standing than does the other. Both needs and wants, while sharing a basis of meaning, part in the popular understanding of each term.

In general, a "want" (which, in general, I would term a "third order necessity") is said to denote something of lesser importance than does a "need": It is more likely to be viewed as the result of idiosyncratic desire, whim, or taste. Wants have more emotive and subjective overtones: I may want a haircut even when I may acknowledge that I really do not or do not as yet need one. A statement of this sort will be quite comprehensible to most people and will not be felt to be internally conflicting. Most persons will understand that my statement that I want a haircut is motivated by personal whim and personal desire (by how I feel rather than by what my appearance really is) rather than being something most outside observers would agree upon. Needing a haircut, however, is something which not only I would feel to be the case but is something that outside observers could, by applying certain criteria, generally agree upon.

Of course, needs and wants can be contrasted in other ways. I may, if "objective" criteria are applied by outside observers, be found to need something that I really do not want: say a haircut or, perhaps, coronary bypass surgery. This may be the case even when I agree to the goal the need subserves (I want to look good or to live longer or to be free of pain), to the criteria, and to their applicability in my case. Often, but not always, I may allow the need rather than the want to control my actions: I may go and get a haircut or have bypass surgery done. But then I would say that I allowed my reason to rule, allowed my head rather than my heart to make the decision, and would then—and not gladly—abide by it. Or I might decide the other way. Whichever was the case, it would be clear that wants and needs may coincide or conflict. Wants and needs clearly are different things. Needs, we might say, are far less subjective than are wants and yet a confusion of terms persists.

Such a confusion of meanings makes the discussion of what constitutes a need and what a (mere) want problematic. A need to one is seen as a want by another: especially when I judge my need vis-à-vis another's supposed (mere) want. As humans we are apt to downplay another's need especially when acknowledging that something to be a need may entail our obligation to meet it. This is readily illustrated in the attitude toward the poor by many of those who are not: What is seen as a need by the poor is often claimed to be a mere want by those who might feel responsible for supplying it if a true need were to be acknowledged. By redefining a previous need and downgrading it to a mere want we try to define our obligations out of existence. Working mothers may see maternity leave or day care for their children as a true need; those who might have to accept the economic consequences of such a decision are apt to see maternity leave for new mothers or day care for their children as a luxury. When a two-tiered system in health care is considered, those who would depend on what is freely available define a need quite differently than do those ultimately responsible for meeting that need. Most will consider private rooms in the hospital or wine with dinner not to be a need; but many will part company when it comes to other matters such as privacy or staffing.

This raises two problems: (1) Are needs, just like wants, purely subjective, purely determinable by those who feel the need, or can needs in some way be objectively or broadly determined? (2) Even if there are criteria by which such an objective determination can be made, are objectively determined needs variable depending upon socially determined factors? In other words, is *objective* here usable in the strictest sense that is realistically possible, or is *objective* broader, more variable, and dependent upon the social and historical setting in which such needs are enunciated?

I shall leave the notion of the difference between needs and wants aside. If one accepts that needs are, in some sense at least, more important than wants, then, when dealing with matters of justice, supplying needs takes precedence over fulfilling mere wants (and, some would claim, fulfilling wants is not even a matter which ordinarily involves considerations of communal justice). Fulfilling every want of every member of a community is impossible; fulfilling critical needs, depending upon the resources of a society and upon their just distribution, may not be. I will attempt to avoid the morass of needs and wants and largely confine the discussion to needs, itself a highly problematic issue. Invariably, issues of allocation emerge from our notion of justice just as our idea of justice is founded on our perception of community and social contract. When dealing with the allocation of resources the language of needs seems unavoidable and a clear idea of what constitutes a need, then, becomes essential. This is so whether the allocation is by one person to another or whether it is by the community to its citizens. And yet, as Daniels has pointed out, the concept of needs is a slippery one.[4]

In popular language a need can be almost anything: a passing fancy ("I need to take a look in this store window"), a desire ("I need to go to concerts"), or a condition of my existence ("I need air!"). Some of these may be classified as wants and others as needs but the ideas share a common root. Derived from its root of necessity, both a need and a want imply that something is required so as to attain a predetermined end. My need to look into the shop window can reasonably be expected to satisfy my curiosity as to what it contains; my need to satisfy my love of music is served by going to (the right kind of) concerts, and my desire to live requires air as a necessary condition. In the sense that the particular action or thing is necessary to attain a given goal, all of these are needs.

Using the term "need" does not indicate the importance of that need in a hierarchy of values. It merely indicates that having or doing a certain thing is a necessary condition if a given goal is to be attained. In order to attain a goal—no matter how lofty or trivial—a certain thing (or action) is necessary. The necessity depends not on the importance or value of the goal but on the importance of the means (the needed thing) to reach the goal. In that sense the term "need" in and of itself does not indicate anything about the nature of the goal. A need, then, is somewhat like the "ought" in a hypothetical. It is an ought which must be fulfilled if the indicated goal is to be reached: If you want to reach $x$ you ought (need) to do or have $y$. As such and in and of itself the term "need" (as the term "ought," when hypothetically used) is essentially value-neutral. It can be applied equally to the despicable (if you want to kill Jones you need—ought—to use poison), as it can to the commendable (if you want to save that child you need—ought—to give her food).

If needs are the necessary condition (the means) to desired ends, they may still not, by themselves, be sufficient to attain those ends. Food, for example, is only one of the necessary conditions for sustaining life: Without it life does not long endure. But food alone does not suffice; other, additional conditions are needed to sustain life. Goals in the real world are often, if not invariably, subserved by composite needs aimed at their fulfillment. This realization often leads to abandoning the attempt to reach a goal: one has often heard that there is no point in feeding the hungry, in providing homes for the homeless, or in serving some other social justice issue. After all, so the argument goes, feeding the hungry by itself does not serve the goal of social justice. Such arguments are specious. While allowing well-fed people to go homeless solves little, it does work significantly toward the overall goal of alleviating suffering.

When I say that needs are a necessary condition to desired ends, I do not mean to imply either that ends are fixed or that a strict separation between means and ends is possible. The condition necessary to attain a desired end (the things that are needed to attain that end) may be a means at one time and may, in the past, have been an end. I need food, water, shelter, and other things to live and such things then are the means directed to the end of being alive. But being alive is, in itself, a means towards yet another end: I need to live so that I may, among other things, have a biography.[5] And having a biography may well be looked upon as a means to yet another end. Means and ends, therefore, are interactive and mutually supportive and corrective: The means I use may change the end I have in mind, and the end may determine the means I use. Ferdinand Lasalle, the great German socialist, put it well: "Show me not the end without the means for in the means the end is written."

Rather than attempting to find one definite and ultimate end, a search which bears a remarkable similarity to the quest for the summum bonum, one can look at the means-and-ends question as one of supporting inquiry. Dewey speaks of this as "ends in view." Ends cannot be established once and for all: Once attained they are likely to become means to yet another end beyond.[5,6,7] Having an end in view helps inquiry (helps, in other words, to make an "indeterminate situation somewhat more determinate") but it does not make the end either fixed or entirely separable from the antecedent means or the inevitable consequences resulting from its selection. Ends and means are on a continuum and not entirely separable from each other.

Human needs, including biological human needs, exist in a social setting and goals are social goals. If modern man is to live in an acceptable manner, rather than merely exist in a biological sense, conditions other than those of strict biological need must be met. Such needs are socially defined. I shall try to show that needs have both a biological and a social basis, will try to define what constitutes a basic need and then will try to subdivide basic needs into what I have called first- and second-order necessities.

Saying that anything (health care, for example, or education or basic nutrition) is or is not a basic need demands further definition. In a sense, going to the opera is a need for many and having at least a little pleasure in life is a need for all. But going to the opera or having a little pleasure in life are different kinds of "needs." Basic needs in this definition are set apart either by being biologically necessary to sustain normal life itself or by being socially necessary to create those conditions which may make life, once established, worth living. Going to the opera is, even though shared by many, a highly personal need, which, for most, serves to embellish life rather than serving a more fundamental need. It is what I call a third-order necessity.

In the vitalist presumption, life itself is a good worth pursuing at all costs. Few would subscribe to this extreme a stand. Those who would subscribe to such a stand are then forced to maintain every spark of organic life no matter what. Those who would not assume the vitalist stance (and, in fact, few of us would), will need to maintain life as the basic condition of experience rather than supporting life merely as an end in itself.[8] Life itself, in such a point of view, is a first-order presumption: a condition for experience; the things that make such living minimally worthwhile are, in that phraseology, second-order presumptions. Meeting first-order necessities is the means subserving the goal of being alive; the goal, once attained and established, now becomes the means (the necessary condition) for leading a full life. Meeting second-order necessities is the means serving that goal which, when once attained, opens a whole new range of possibilities and goals.

Some may argue that under the above definition, health care, as it pertains to the saving of life, even if not to the amelioration of suffering, is a first-order necessity. Such an argument has substance but it fails to differentiate between primitive existence (subserved by meeting such needs as food and water) and needs which are seen as needs only because man has learned to foil nature's threats. Such needs are the product of civilized living in a sense which air, water, food, shelter and warmth are not. For the sake of discussion, I am quite willing to grant that health care as well as education are not needs in the same sense that needs underwriting mere existence are; what I am quite unwilling to grant is that, therefore, a just community has little or no obligation to see to it that such needs are met.

When Daniels speaks of health care as necessary to "provide individuals with access to a normal opportunity range consistent with the pursuit of an array of life plans which reasonable persons are likely to construct for themselves," he gives one of the main reasons why, in a modern society, health care is such a second-order necessity.[4] Without meeting second-order needs, first-order necessities are empty; second-order necessities are meaningless without initially satisfying those of the first order.

The relationship between basic first- and basic second-order necessities is quite analogous to the relationship between social justice and individual rights. Ontologically, first-order necessities must be met for any individual before he can take advantage of those of the second order. In a similar manner, having one's first-order needs met is quite empty unless some of the other needs of social existence are readily available. The end of living (underwritten by the means of meeting first-order needs) becomes a means for attaining the new ends of having access to a full opportunity range; in turn, the end of attaining access now becomes a means towards living a full and satisfying life. Ends are not fixed and as they are attained they easily become the means towards another "end in view."

Education has a quite similar standing. Without sufficient education, access to a full opportunity range which reasonable (and talented) individuals may have for themselves is precluded. Persons with the capacity to teach, heal, or extend the frontiers of the unknown may, instead, be selling neckties or collecting garbage. This, of course, is not only harmful to the individual but is destructive for the community which ultimately derives its robustness from the developed talents of its members. Furthermore, such individuals, frustrated and unsatisfied, are apt to feel little solidarity with their community. The community which fails to offer treatment for treatable illness or education for remediable ignorance and the full flourishing of talents not only lacks compassion but does itself a disservice and shatters solidarity.

In delineating needs beyond first-order needs, then, the social context becomes all important. Even among the Ba Mbuti living their traditional life, there are needs beyond those that merely sustain life: but these further needs are obviously different from those of highly organized and industrialized societies. To realize access to a normal opportunity range consistent with the pursuit of an array of life plans which reasonable persons are likely to construct for themselves among the Ba Mbuti (or among the ancient Greeks, among medieval European peasants or among the twenty-fifth-century inhabitants of Greenland) is a different matter than doing so in Moscow, New York, or Tientsin today. Although first-order necessities remain essentially stable throughout these societies, it is the social context which fashions the things we legitimately may want to call second-order necessities and those to which we may deny such a standing. Except for the biological needs of first-order necessities, other needs and their prioritization are a social construct and not one which can be settled for all times or all places.

This leaves unsettled what to include and what to exclude among this category of second-order needs: a category meant to include those things required to sustain at least minimally acceptable existence within a given social context so that reasonable individual goals can be met. The definition hinges on what is acceptable or reasonable as a goal within a given context.

Some will say that "acceptable" and "reasonable" are terms which are so subjective and so idiosyncratic as to defy definition. I maintain that what is and what is not acceptable or reasonable within a given society or context is a decision which can only be made by the community which forms the society or context. There are no discoverable (or none yet discovered!) precise or explicit criteria which can govern such a definition. Communities will have to make such decisions by a democratic process in which informed and interested members all participate. And to participate requires, at the very least, basic health and basic education to understand and deal with such problems. Communities which meet basic second-order needs hardly profit only those to whom they are supplied: They profit the community which needs basically healthy and happy members to assure its own present solidarity as well as its continuity and progress.

How does one circumscribe a second-order necessity? We have said that education and health care are two examples of such necessities; do we mean all health care and all education, or just some, and then how do we determine the extent? If we define such second-order necessities in the way Professor Daniels does (as things which are necessary to give individuals a decent chance to realize an array of life plans reasonable within that community[4]) a start can be made. One can, for example, argue that becoming a physician, an attorney, a housewife, a nurse, a philosopher, or an academic, are, given the necessary native ability, not unreasonable ambitions in our particular society and that they are well within the scope of "reasonable arrays" in a way in which having opera tickets is generally not. Should we agree to this, providing an opportunity to go to professional schools or receive other training (an opportunity limited only by personal ability and not by economic circumstances) fulfills a second-order need; it will be argued later, that the fulfillment of second-order needs, once first-order needs have been met and within the limits of its resources, is an obligation of a just society.

But is health care (or education) too broad a concept? Are we obligated to meet to its full extent the World Health Organization (WHO) definition (which defines health as "a state of complete, physical, mental and social well-being and not merely the absence of disease and infirmity"[9]) or to supply all members with limitless education? In pursuing our argument as it relates to health care, and while using the WHO definition as an ideal, we are after smaller game. As it pertains to health care, the spectrum of considerations in our definition of needs should provide procedures to: 1) save life; 2) ameliorate pain; 3) restore the function of vital parts; and 4) prevent future problems by public health, immunization, and other forms of preventive medicine. Saving life can be argued to be almost a first-order need. Without life our plans are at an end. And if life is protected, pain significantly interferes with our ability to pursue life's plans; when chronic it may thwart them altogether. The function of vital parts (be they parts which underwrite life—hearts or livers—or parts which are necessary for optimal function—corneas or legs) likewise is necessary to achieve our reasonable desires. Preventing future problems by preventive medicine not only obviates the need for other interventions but in itself may significantly add to a person's security and wellbeing thus enabling her to go freely about her business. Health itself is not, nor can ever be, a right. To be healthy requires much, much more than health care or social conditions: It requires also, among other things, a bit of luck. But adequate health and the opportunity, when that is possible, to be healthy is most assuredly and at the very least a second-order need in modern society.

In necessarily supporting access to a full opportunity range, education has a quite similar standing. Like health care, being well educated depends upon more than opportunity for education. It too depends upon a bit of luck in having the proper mind to be developed as well as the support of family or friends who hold education in high esteem. Adequate education—adequate so that individuals may develop their minds to the full extent allowed by their particular luck—is most assuredly also a second-order necessity in modern society, and some education is necessary to achieve the goals of any society. The type of education needed by the Ba Mbuti to obtain full access to the opportunities of their particular society may be starkly different from that needed in Sweden today, but education of some type is still needed. Education, in point of fact, may be a more basic second-order need than is health care. With some luck, people may need little health care for many years and be able to achieve their goals independent of it. That cannot be said of education, the lack of or opportunity for which, from the very beginning, constricts or opens their opportunity range.

The details of this (what, for example, is health? or what is it to be educated adequately to provide access to a full opportunity range?) would be subject to the political process and would be a growing and ever changing consideration adjudicated by the community.[10] Inasmuch as the definitions of disease as well as the conditions to be met in being adequately educated are a social construct,[3,11,13] the definition of health (or adequate education to achieve a given goal) is a social construct, and is viewed quite differently in different communities and at different times. Health care (just as education), as the activity which promotes health and opposes disease (or sufficient education to pursue certain goals), can be seen as directed in its definition by the community in which it is rooted.[10] The specifics of what constitutes necessary health care will vary from community to community and from time to time and it will be dependent upon prevalent communal values. Communities, for example, that place a very high value on beauty, and in which a high degree of comeliness is necessary to the attainment of life plans considered as reasonable within that community, will be more inclined than others to include certain forms of plastic surgery in their array of procedures concerned with health care.

It is interesting that education and health care have always been seen as quite similar needs. In the nineteenth century, conservatives in England were arguing against the merits of state education in almost the same language as was to be used in America a hundred years later in combating the notion of health care under the sponsorship of the state. Those opposing (as well as those proposing) the idea couched their views in almost identical language.[13]

There are other ways of examining needs. Rights, according to some, are grounded in human needs. If rights are acknowledged to be grounded in human needs, some claim that there is no stopping short of a radical Marxism,[14] which wishes to give "to each according to need" and to extract from each "according to ability."[15] Those who argue for a decent minimum of health care (or education) as a human right hew to a similar line.[10,16] Churchill, in his important book, grounds the ethical right to health care in human need, in a social concept of the self, in a common humanity, and in a knowledge of common vulnerability to disease and death.[17] He grapples with the notion of needs, acknowledging that the concept of need will "founder so long as it is individually defined." Needs, in Churchill's view, are individual but they are socially defined and validated. So, for that matter, is education. Health care, as Norman Daniels has said, is "important to maintaining normal species function." Health care in that view is an instrumental right, not as important in itself as it is important in underwriting other ends (autonomous function, for example) which we also value.[17] In the view expressed here, health care is important because of the goal that it subserves: It is not a first-order need for it is not needed to underwrite basic and primitive biological function, but it (like education) is a second-order need, one which, in modern society, is necessary to sustain acceptable existence within a given social context so that reasonable individual goals can be met.

Health care (or education) serves a far deeper human purpose than underwriting the immensely important access to a full opportunity range which reasonable persons may desire. Health care serves a purpose directly concerned with elemental human facts: with suffering, with birth and death, with grief and joy. These facts are buried in the very marrow of human existence, transcend most societal norms, and are far more than merely material conditions allowing access. Education is likewise concerned with elemental human facts: with removing terror through understanding, with meeting the very human need of explaining, and with adaptation to the physical and social environment. Education, as well as health care, are needed to deal appropriately with suffering, birth, death, grief, and joy.[18]

When I have used the terms "needs" or "basic needs," I have been concerned with first or second-order needs. First-order needs, as I have pointed out, are natural needs which are purely biological and which are needs because they underpin bare biological existence. Unless they are met, biological existence cannot continue. I have argued and, in what is to follow will continue to maintain, that wherever possible, just communities are obligated to meet such needs before meeting the less crucial ones of others within the community. Meeting first-order needs is the first order of business in a community which bases its vision of justice on more than on mere mutual nonharm and concerns itself with the wellbeing—and not only with the freedom—of its members. Communities which recognize beneficent obligations and who define justice as entailing other obligations than merely those of mutual nonharm will not willingly stand by and allow some members to live luxuriously while others perish for want of bare necessities. As long as some starve or have other unmet first-order needs, just communities will feel compelled to limit the luxurious consumption of a few and will feel entitled to take some of the riches from the wealthiest to benefit those who are in want.

In what is to come, I shall argue that communities which have provided members with the first-order necessities essential for maintaining biological existence are further compelled, if possible, to meet second-order needs as defined within the community before concerning themselves with third-order needs, which are less compelling. Such needs are less compelling because they are connected with far less elemental facts of human existence. When we see people starving to death or see them homeless (when, in other words, their first-order needs have not been met) our natural sense of compassion is aroused. We see such a state of affairs as a problem not just of sociology or economics but one which has become a question of ethics. When we see sick people who are suffering, our natural sense of compassion is likewise aroused and we hope that medical science might be able to affect a cure or, at least, to ameliorate their suffering. When we see capable men and women unable to reach their full flowering and unable to express their talents because education was unavailable, we likewise feel a deep sense of compassion. If, in addition, we find out that access to medical care is not available because such persons are poor and uninsured or that education, while available, was not available to them because they lacked the necessary funds, our compassion with their plight leads us to see such a state of affairs as an ethical problem for our community. In a sense we see them as having been wronged.

Needs are bio-socially conditioned: *biologically* in that biology underpins all social structures and *socially* in that the specifics of needs are set by and in communities and, therefore, will vary according to time and place. When communities strive for a balance between individual freedom and values they will recognize justice (giving others their due) as consisting not only of nonharm but equally as necessitating beneficent obligations. A balance of this sort recognizes that social justice is prior to individual rights: The hungry and homeless are rarely comforted by the thought that they have the freedom to assemble. But it also recognizes that, while social justice is the necessary basis for individual liberties, it is empty without it. Having enough to eat and having shelter is necessary if we are to enjoy the fruits of individual liberties, but having enough to eat and having shelter is meaningless and empty unless such liberties can be attained. Communities which recognize this will try to meet first-order needs, thus providing an existence for all prior to meeting second-order needs. And they will try to provide basic second-order necessities for all members prior to allowing other members to enjoy opulent private luxuries. Should communities have sufficient resources so that the basic needs of all are met with still large resources left to spare, meeting third-order needs may become a community issue, but in our world today, this is hardly the case! A careful definition of needs underpins the way we view allocation issues.

## References

1. Oakshott M: *On Human Conduct*. Oxford: Clarendon Pres, 1975.

2. Douart J: Ethics, AIDS and Community Responsibility. *Theoretical Med.* 1990 (in publication).

3. Engelhardt HT: *The Foundations of Bioethics*. New York: Oxford University Press, 1986.

4. Daniels N: *Just Health Care*. New York: Cambridge University Press, 1985.

5. Rachels J: *The End of Life*. New York: Oxford University Press, 1986.

6. Dewey J: *Ethics*. New York: Henry Holt and Company, 1932.

7. Dewey J: Means and Consequences—How, What and What For. In *Dewey J, Bentley AF: A Philosophical Correspondence, 1932-1951*. Ratner, S. and J. Altman, eds. New Brunswick, NJ: Rutgers University Press, 1964.

8. Loewy EH: Treatment Decisions in the Mentally Impaired: Limiting but not Abandoning Treatment. *NEJM 317*(23):1465-69, 1987.

9. World Health Organization: Constitution of the World Health Organization 22 July 1946. *Publ Hlth Rep 61*:1268-71, 1946.

10. Loewy EH: Communities, Obligations and Health Care. *Soc Sci & Med* 25(7):783-91, 1987.

11. Engelhardt HT: The Disease of Masturbation: Values and the Concept of Disease. *Bull Hist of Med 48*:234-48, 1974.

12. Burnum JF: Medical Practice a la Mode: How Medical Fashions Determine Medical Care. *NEJM 317*(19):1220-22, 1987.

13. Heeney B: Opposition to State Medicine and State Education: An Historical Analogy. *Queens Q 75*:72-89, 1968.

14. Singer P: Freedom and Utilities in the Distribution of Health Care. In *Ethics and Health Policy*. By R. Veatch and R. Branson. Cambridge: Ballinger, 1976.

15. Marx K: *The Communist Manifesto*. New York: Washington Square Press, 1965.

16. Fried C: An Analysis of 'Equality' and 'Rights' in Medical Care. In *Ethical Issues in Modern Medicine*, 2nd Ed. By J. Arras and R. Hunt. Palo Alto, CA: Mayfield Publishers, 1983.

17. Churchill L: *Rationing Health Care in America: Perceptions and Principles of Justice*. Notre Dame IN: University of Notre Dame Press, 1987.

18. Loewy EH: Communities, Entrepreneurialism and Health Care. In *The Clinical Relationship: Towards a Hermeneutical Perspective*. D. Schultz and G. Sherlock eds. Indianapolis: University of Indiana Press, 1989.

# Chapter Six

# Limits

An ethic grounded in the capacity of sentient beings to suffer, and a notion of community which sees obligations as far richer than merely refraining from harming others and envisions solidarity as inevitably linked to mutual beneficence, must nevertheless confront a world in which resources are not infinite. Therefore, limits to the use of those resources must be set. Our response to the realization that limits exist is properly a careful allocation of these resources so that they can be wisely and optimally used to further private or communal values. It does not matter if limited resources are material or are, like time, non-material: Once it is recognized and acknowledged that a resource is limited, we must either learn to extend the limit or we must adapt ourselves to such a limit by prudent use of the limited resource. These are not mutually exclusive strategies: We may adapt ourselves to what we recognize as today's limits while attempting (by thought or action) to push our limits further. Most of us have a limited income: Working within a budget so as not to go into debt and trying to extend the limit by increasing our income are not mutually exclusive.

Limits may be actual: they may be "out there," immutable and unchanging. But our recognition of what is and what is not limited and the nature of such a limitation is not equivalent to the actuality or fact of such finitude. To state that limits exist is a far different thing than to claim knowledge of precisely those limits are. Similar to Kant's phenomena and noumena, the "thing in itself" ("das Ding an Sich"), the noumenon, may exist, but we, in the human condition, can only recognize its phenomenal appearance.[1] We may recognize the fact that limits exist while claiming that we cannot know precisely what these limits are or how far such limits may, by our own action, be extended. Working to extend our limits beyond what they are today is by no means inconsistent with believing that ultimately we may not be able to extend them.

We may acknowledge theoretical limits while, at the same time, claiming that knowing precisely what these limits are is, in the human condition, uncertain and imprecise. Or we may advance the claim that we can either discover what these limits are or that we are empowered to artificially set such limits. These are quite different claims: The discovering of limits suggests the absolutist claim that not only does truth exist but that truth is humanly discoverable; setting limits is an acknowledgement that under certain circumstances limits on human activities must be set for the common good. Such a claim is a social claim grounded in the utility which setting such limits is believed to have.

The more absolutist claim is one which pretends to discover (or, at times, to have discovered) such limits. In a secular framework such limits will be called "natural"; in a religious framework, they are apt to be called "divine." The idea is not so much that we can or should set limits as that such natural (or divine) limits simply exist, need to be and can be discovered (or to be revealed), and that we, in the human condition, need to shape our policies and adapt our actions to what "is the case." On the other hand, a more social claim either denies the existence of limits or, if acknowledging them, denies our ability to discover them. The social claim will then cautiously attempt to set certain limits based on reason, empirical evidence, and social utility. Such limits will, consequently, not be held to be immutable nor will experimentation to extend the limits be necessarily precluded. Empirical evidence, human knowledge, and social conditions all change and, according to this point of view limits will have to change likewise. Unless experimentation continues at the fringes of these limits, pressing to extend them, no one can legitimately determine whether they are or are not extensible.

Setting a speed limit is an example. We find that our cars can be safely operated at a certain speed and that our consumption of fuel at such a speed is likewise reasonable. The amount of fuel consumed at a given speed by a given car will be an empirical observation; what is and what is not considered to be a reasonable consumption of fuel or what is and what is not reasonable safety is a communal judgment based on values and reason. A speed is then chosen by the community, but as empirical evidence continues to accumulate (the speed chosen may not be reasonably safe or new advances in the automotive industry may allow greater fuel economy at higher speeds), the limit is changed. Beyond this, communal values change in accord with changing conditions: A reasonable consumption of fuel when fuel is inexpensive and readily available is quite different from one when fuel is in short supply and expensive. Likewise what is and what is not accepted as reasonable safety may change as communal values evolve.

There are far more critical but equally changeable limits. Certain human cancers only a few years ago limited the life spans of their victims. Realistically, only comfort could be offered to such patients whose lives were inevitably coming to an end. The wise and compassionate physician would not insist on futile and unwanted treatment. But in many cases such limits have changed: Many forms of cancer have a high likelihood of cure and no longer constitute the limit to medical practice that they once did. Research to extend what was once a limit has allowed many who would otherwise be dead or dying to live productive and healthy lives. Of course, one could have set limits before this; one could have said that developing leukemia, Hodgkins, or choriocarcinoma was a natural limit and one which it was either useless or not our business to change.

Human history has been full of limits which once were seen as insuperable but which were overcome. Humanity learned to use fire, to make clothing, to pour cement, to fly (and, unfortunately, to make horrible weapons). Lower animals, not having a transmittable history, have more rigid limits than do humans. But even the limits imposed on lower animals change: Individual animals may learn (by what amounts to experimentation) to overcome limits for themselves and changes in the material and social conditions of the animal environment may further modify and change such limits. Wherever we look, we see that limits change and evolve as material or social conditions, understanding, and, consequently, our abilities change.

In this chapter I will develop a theory of limits which sees limits as empirically determined but only determinable for a given time and place. In the past, we died when we had certain diseases, and in that same past we were unable to fly: Those were limits then. Today we can cure some of those diseases and have learned to fly. Our limits are different now. This chapter will oppose the notion which Daniel Callahan puts forth in his two recent books: Limits are not only "setable" now but are "setable" now for the future.[2,3] It will deal briefly with how the setting of limits is an ongoing experimental and evolutionary activity and not a final or determinable endpoint. Medicine will be used as an example of such an activity and the important difference between therapeusis and experimentation will be sketched.

It is unclear whether Callahan believes that limits are discoverable or that we must set them. In many ways, Callahan suggests both. On the one hand, he speaks of a natural lifespan, which suggests a more absolutist perception; on the other, he speaks of "setting" limits. If, indeed, there is such a natural lifespan and if, which is not the same thing, we have somehow been able to discover what such a lifespan is, setting limits makes no sense: They have been set for us. If, on the other hand, there is either no natural lifespan, if what is natural does not really greatly matter, or if we, in the human condition, cannot discover what the natural lifespan is, then arbitrarily setting such a span takes on different overtones. In the first case, experimenting to extend these limits makes no sense: Limits have been set for us. In the other case (if, in fact, these are human-made instead of natural limits) stopping experimentation to extend such limits creates a circular and rigid situation: We artificially and arbitrarily decide what constitutes a limit and then create a self-fulfilling prophecy by enforcing what we have artificially and arbitrarily set.

The problem I will deal with in this chapter is not specifically the problem of using age as a limiting factor. I have, as we shall see later on, severe theoretical as well as practical problems with such a notion. The problems I want to deal with are (1) the belief that natural limits are either discoverable or, indeed, that what is natural should greatly matter, and (2) the very notion that it is ethically permissible, if not indeed desirable, to set arbitrary limits on the allocation of basic necessities and even to fix such limits by stopping experimentation to extend them. Callahan advances the claim that setting limits has merit because it provides a boundary and "forces a facing up to the course of a life and to the fact that it exists within a finite length of time."[2] Limits, not only the limits which our "natural lifespan" imposes but the very notion of limits can, according to Callahan, provide a certain amount of comfort in realizing the finitude of one's framework as one goes about one's business.[2,3]

Knowing that limits exist may, in fact, be comforting. Children and infants certainly need a framework within which they can operate and which, by its very being, adds to their security. Part of growing up, however, is a constant testing and expanding of the limits which such a framework provides. Education, in many ways, consists of allowing children to expand the framework (to "stretch their limits" and to exert their autonomy in the embrace of beneficence) until the external framework falls away and a self-imposed framework takes its place. Such an experience is similar to the process of self-legislation in which, according to Kant, persons are worthy of respect because they are "autonomous" beings capable of self-legislation, providing, as it were, their own framework and limits.[4] Self-legislation also takes place in the embrace of a beneficent community: Proper self-legislation occurs within a social framework and is mindful of the needs of others. Internally applied limits are far different than those imposed by others. External limits or frameworks do, of course, exist. Physical frameworks (the material and biological conditions in which we operate and which our free will accepts as its limit of action), of course, are real. The only way, however, in which we can recognize such a limit is by testing it, manipulating it, and, if possible, shaping or extending it to suit our purpose.

I have no quarrel with the notion that natural limits exist. The world and its resources are obviously finite and only a fool would argue with such a proposition. I do have serious problems with the notions that: (1) natural limits matter under all and every circumstance; (2) they are discoverable by us for all times and are unchangeable; (3) they can be arbitrarily set for critical matters, especially for basic human needs; and (4) attempts to increase human knowledge so that current limits can be extended should be arbitrarily stopped. Using medicine as a paradigm, I want to examine the notion of natural limits.

That natural limits exist is beyond all doubt. Some limits, at least in our current state of knowledge, seem to be limits beyond our ability to do anything about. The fact that nothing can travel beyond the speed of light and that, therefore, the speed of light constitutes a limiting condition for the speed of travel appears (at least for the state of our knowledge today) a well-accepted proposition. There are, however, other limits which were seen as limits yesterday and which today have been left far behind. I think here of some of the many limits imposed by the state of our knowledge and our understanding. Such things as the fact that we could not fly or cure certain diseases were indisputably limits at one time but are not today. Furthermore, such limits were quite natural: It required human understanding and manipulation of nature to extend these limits and to move beyond.

There are even more primitive natural limits imposed, for example, by climactic conditions. One cannot live at very low temperatures without using clothing, shelter, and fire. Such primitive innovations extended man's ability to live and function under otherwise hostile conditions. We have never accepted the natural limits imposed by environmental conditions as human destiny. And, for that matter, manipulating nature is by no means unique to our species. The higher animals do not necessarily accept the limits of nature but attempt to adapt (even if primitively) their environment so that natural obstacles can be overcome. Primitive tools (used by some primates as well as by other animals) extend the limits imposed by nature.

While obvious limits exist they are often only limits as we perceive them in our particular and peculiar moment in time and place. Our perception depends upon the way in which we understand nature and nature's laws. They are not fixed and immutable or, if they are, we cannot know this. For our practical purposes, limits are empirically determined and socially validated: We know we cannot (today) cure AIDS or (today) jump over tall buildings; we knew (yesterday) that we could not cure plague or fly. Our methods of validating empirical facts are social: We agree that certain observed phenomena constitute proof and that others do not. Limits can be determined by and for us in relation to what we socially perceive to be the limits of the possible, but what is and what is not possible is determined by the extent of our knowledge. Setting limits on extending limits and saying "thus far and no further" is basically either an arbitrary statement precluding possibilities for tomorrow, or it is a statement of incredible hubris advancing the claim that we, today, are the apex of creation and that no more than what we already know can be known and no more than what we are already doing possibly can or ought to be accomplished.

Dealing with the notion of limits is crucial if we are to deal with a beneficent community truly concerned about the suffering of its members. I have argued previously that meeting the basic needs of their individual members is an obligation of beneficent communities. Meeting basic needs is done so that suffering can be minimized. If resources were truly unlimited and freely available no suffering caused by a lack of available resources would exist. If, however, we accept the notion that limits are fixed, attempting to extend them is either foolish because such limits constitute a given of nature or not allowable by our social rules. Accepting the normative values such a notion implies, forces us into accepting the status quo and makes evolution beyond such predetermined borders impossible.

Extremely paternalistic communities, like communities which are extremely autonomy-based, will be likely to embrace the notion of limits to achieve quite different (but in their effect quite similar) ends: Paternalist communities will be apt to impose severe limits on freedom of action; autonomy-based communities will limit the contributions to beneficence individuals can be compelled to give. Consequently such communities will be able to discharge only the most minimal beneficent obligations. In the paternalistic community, the framework is likely to inhibit the flourishing of individual talents and tastes; in the autonomy-based community, the autonomy of some individuals severely limits the ability of others to live or enjoy a full life. Setting limits almost invariably restricts autonomy. The types of limits we set provide another example of the dialectic between beneficence and autonomy.

When one allows a strong preponderance of one over the other, rather than striving for a dynamic balance, a very similar final state of affairs results.

I first of all want to deny that what is conceived as a natural limit matters when it comes to setting policy or to extending knowledge. Unless we are to appeal to divine inspiration, it is not possible for us to know what such limits are without experimentation to extend them. If we look at limits as absolutes, then all efforts at overcoming them will cease. The fact that a limit is a limit becomes self-validating: The fact that we recognize (or arbitrarily establish) a limit is used as a proper reason not to extend it and as proof that it cannot be extended. Viewing today's obvious limits as absolutes (as givens to which we simply must adapt, not as obstacles which we must somehow learn to overcome) forces us into a blind acceptance of the status quo and precludes progress. Saying that we ought not to experiment in order to gain new knowledge and understanding is deriving an "ought" from an "is." I do not deny that "is" and "ought" are related; I do deny—and shall spend little time arguing—that what is has normative meaning for what ought to be. Unless we strain against today's limits, unless we think, experiment, and strive, we cannot know whether nature and what is natural can be adapted and, eventually, overcome.

We need to be clear what is meant by the idea of "natural" and, consequently, what is meant by "natural limits." If "natural" implies our material universe and if "natural limits" are those imposed by the material conditions of the universe, then, of course, the material conditions do, in some sense, constitute limits. But the sense in which these material conditions constitute limits is neither clear nor immutable. No one truly believes that nature and its ways constitutes a normative force. Not only human but animal existence is a constant straining against natural forces, sometimes bending them to one's purpose, other times overcoming them. The issue is not one of blindly overcoming nature, not one of seeing in nature an enemy or an obstacle. The issue is to recognize that whatever nature is, it is malleable by our understanding. Nature can be viewed as an opportunity rather than as an obstacle: It is the material for our thoughts and actions. To hold that the material (nature) we work with ultimately constitutes the limit of our ability to shape it is to acknowledge a truth, but to hold that this material (nature) as we now see it cannot be shaped in many ways other than the ways we have so far discovered and that, therefore, the *ways in which we have shaped it* and not the material itself are the limit, is to confuse the material with what we make of it. What is natural is nature, not what we have made of it. If we look at a piece of material (or at a bit of knowledge), we can see in it either the objects (or ideas) we have shaped with it in the past and claim that this limits future use to what has so far been accomplished; or we can see in that material an almost unlimited opportunity for fashioning other objects (or ideas). Humanity advances when it seeks innovative ways of shaping the material given by nature; it stagnates and inevitably backslides when it stops doing this. All of history proves that point.

If it is true that nature is the material with which we must work and which we must shape, and that the extent of our ability to work and shape it in different ways is unknown and unknowable, then what is natural matters only insofar as it presents us with today's challenge for tomorrow. Falling back on a claim that something that is natural constitutes a barrier which we either cannot (or ought not) to overcome is to flee into a conservatism inimical to all positive change. It locks what can be in the future into what has been the case in the past.

As I understand Callahan, he does not go quite that far. He limits his desire to set such limits, and his obeisance to what is natural, to our span of life. That, of course, is entirely arbitrary: Why should a natural span of life have normative force while the natural course of a curable disease or the natural obstacles created by some law of nature (say, gravity) do not? Once we acknowledge that arbitrary limits of this sort can or ought to be set, we open a Pandora's box.

Societies do have to set certain limits. Setting limits on absolute freedom is acknowledged even by libertarians: They would limit the exercise of personal freedom when it threatens to limit the freedom of another. Beneficent communities will set stricter limits: They would limit personal freedom not only to prevent harm to others but also, at times, to benefit others. Since I have consistently argued for a community based on a dialectic between autonomy and beneficence and, indeed, for a community in which significant beneficent obligations exist, I have no quarrel with the careful setting of certain temporary, socially conditioned, and not immutable limits. What I object to is the notion that what is indeed natural (i.e., what is the ultimate limiting condition nature imposes) is either known or knowable or that what is today considered to be natural can be allowed to determine the limits we set. The speed with which we drive (or are allowed to drive) our car or the income we make, is not determinable within a natural framework and yet society feels entitled to set such limits. "Natural" as a normative feature usable either to set practical (for example, therapeutic) limits or as a concept limiting our quest for further understanding (for example, by setting limits on experimentation) seems to lack validity as a reason for enunciating limits.

If one cannot use what is and what is not natural as a reason for setting limits (if natural limits either do not exist or are unknowable) and if limits must be set, we seem to be lost on a sea of socially determined relativism in which there are few apparent guideposts. Such a claim, supporting the use of so-called natural limits, appeals to those who believe in a discoverable (rather than in a socially created) ethic, who find comfort in strictly enunciable and enunciated principles, and who, therefore, seek to discover (or claim to have discovered) such an ethic. I shall claim that when limits must be set they are set by a community mindful of its material conditions as well as of its social contract and, therefore, of its values. Communities whose resources are finite are forced (unless they want to close their eyes entirely) to set limits cautiously based on available empirical evidence as well as on social utility. Limits, as we can know them, are social constructs. They are artificially set on the basis of the best information available and are limits set on courses of practical action. When information, social circumstances, or material conditions change, such limits likewise will have to change. Refusing to test the limits by limiting experimentation aimed at that end locks the future into a framework determined by the present.

Setting limits to the speed with which we drive our cars or even to the amount we may earn is a far different matter than limiting our ability to decrease suffering, cure illness, or live to a ripe and functional old age. Limits are socially set by the members of the community for and in which they are set. Since limits must be set, since a community in which all are free to pursue their own individual goals, mindful only not to bring direct injury on others, is a community which ultimately must destroy itself,[5] ways of setting limits need to be determined.

There are different types of limits. We may set a limit on what can be done today without stopping to search for ways of extending such a limit tomorrow. Setting limits on what we may do today, if well done, may be a simple acknowledgment of the facts as they appear to us today: Often it is an act of wisdom. On the other hand, setting limits on examining or extending the very limits we have set, is quite another matter.

When it comes to setting limits on the use of resources, a notion of critical needs and of the structure of the community allocating such resources will help define the ethical dimension of such a task. Communities who strive for a balance between the obligations of beneficence (communal obligations) and the desire for autonomy (individual rights) rather than committing themselves strongly to one or the other side will define their tasks quite differently than those which fail to strive for such a balance or whose balance is severely tilted in one direction. I have argued that, at the very least, communities which acknowledge beneficent obligations must fulfill the first-order needs of their members. These needs, it will be remembered, are those underwriting basic biological existence: food, water, shelter, and other primitive biological requirements needed to sustain life. Further, I have argued that socially defined second-order necessities (those needed to enable persons access to a fair opportunity range, to which reasonable persons might aspire in the context of a given society) must be provided to all members of a community taking beneficent obligations seriously before allowing a few members the private enjoyment of opulent luxuries.

Such considerations may help in setting limits. Setting limits on the right of all members of a community to share in equal access to those basic things needed to sustain existence (first-order necessities) does not jibe with the definition of justice in a community accepting beneficent obligations. Communities with any sense of beneficence will readily acknowledge that they cannot set limits on the right of all members to share in sufficient first-order necessities to sustain existence. By the very definition of what constitutes such needs, unless they are met, individuals will die. Provided they have sufficient resources, communities which see beneficence as a serious obligation and who, therefore, are concerned with the weal and woe of every member, cannot preclude the chance for experience to any member who has the capacity for and who desires such experience. Such communities cannot force their members to continue living or to avail themselves of available necessities, but such communities are bound to do more than merely see to it that none are physically hindered from access. Just communities, defining justice in terms of beneficence rather than merely in terms of autonomy, will have to facilitate the access of their members to first-order necessities. Unless resources are so very limited that even those things needed to sustain life are in critically short supply, communities will avoid setting limits so that any members of the community have no access to first-order necessities, those things needed to sustain life in its more primitive forms.

There is more to life than having one's basic first-order needs met so that one's biological existence can continue. Biological existence is valued by most of us not as a good in itself but as an instrumental good allowing us to strive for other goals. Each community is different in the precise nature of what it may consider as reasonable goals, but all communities explicitly or tacitly realize that such goals exist. Life, liberty, and the pursuit of happiness are in hierarchical order: We cannot have liberty without life and we cannot pursue happiness unless we are alive and free to do so. Once human beings are assured of the things needed to sustain life, they will legitimately strive for those things which make living worthwhile.

The ability to strive for what are considered to be reasonable goals within a given social framework is underwritten by having first-order needs met. But truly having access to a meaningful life (in the sense of access which sees access as more than just not having one's way barred) implies the meeting of other socially defined needs which I have called "second-order needs." For a society taking beneficence seriously, meeting such needs (those which make access to a socially defined "reasonable opportunity range" possible) becomes the next order of business once first-order necessities are assured. Setting limits on meeting second-order needs may well have to be done by societies whose resources are severely taxed and in which no one is enjoying tremendous luxuries and wealth while others are denied the resources needed to attain a reasonable opportunity range. Beneficent societies, which see justice as entailing some beneficent obligations, will set limits on the luxurious living of some before choosing to set such limits on the ability of others to achieve a fair "opportunity range." Further, when societies finally set limits on things which belong to the variety of second-order necessities recognized by it, they will not only allow but perhaps even encourage trials at the fringes of these limits to find ways of extending them. When communities cannot adequately meet the second-order needs of all members and when some must go without just and facilitated access to a full opportunity range, such communities will have a sense of unease and guilt. This sense, originating in compassion for the plight of others, will stimulate communities to experiment with ways of stretching their limits. Even when such communities set limits on what they can do today, they will seek ways of doing better tomorrow. If one accepts, for example, that resources for health care or for education are ultimately limited (as indeed on at least theoretical grounds one must), one will accept that certain forms of health care or education are, as things stand, too costly to be provided. Such a decision, however, does not imply that ways of extending the limits should not be sought. Truly beneficent and compassionate communities will not only try to ameliorate the suffering of their members with the resources available to them but will also try to extend their future beneficence so that more can benefit and benefit more extensively tomorrow than they did today. This is as true for small communities as it is for large ones, and, ultimately, it is true for what has aptly been called the "global village." Beneficent and compassionate communities will attempt to extend their currently perceived limits and work toward a better understanding of the problems and of the solutions possible so that more can be done for all.

Stopping experimentation to stretch limits can be done in two ways. We can (1) stop funding experiments to supply more or to supply more efficiently and broadly the things considered basic necessities, and we can (2) stop funding the ability of members of the community to participate in the consumption of such necessities. These are not the same thing. When we restrict research into new ways of growing food, new ways of treating illness, or new ways of teaching our young we do a different thing than when we restrict research to broaden the base of consumers. We broaden the base of consumers when we judge that others besides those we include today may legitimately receive food, medicine, or education. Experimentation to extend the lifespan offers a fine example. People who live longer and are more functional in old age continue as consumers of first- and second-order necessities. Precluding experiments aimed at doing this keeps the base of consumers artificially narrow. It determines that basic needs (at least second-order needs) no longer apply to such an age group or other arbitrarily determined group. Furthermore the decision not to experiment with extending the lifespan keeps the base of consumers stable.

The net result of stopping funding of experimentation to stretch our limits (be they the limits of what may be available to consume or the limits of who may be entitled to consume) is the same. In one way or another the future is held hostage to the present. The decision that first- or second-order necessities must no longer be distributed to an arbitrarily chosen group who could profit from such a distribution, and the decision that no attempts to enlarge the group itself, eventually arrive at a very similar endpoint.

One can use Professor Callahan's book as an example of the notion that not only must limits on current usage be set but that it is legitimate to set such limits on experimentation aimed at extending what are perceived to be today's limits: either the limits of what may be available or limits of the consumer base. My disagreement transcends the issue of setting limits on treatment merely by virtue of age. I strongly disagree that age alone is a morally acceptable criterion for limiting health care. I do so because age, while having the beauty of being easy to determine, says little else of moral or even of functional relevance about the individual classified in that way, because arbitrarily forbidding access to things needed to extend life shatters solidarity, and because doing so is a serious infringement on access to second-order necessities for some while others continue to enjoy luxuries far beyond reasonable second-order needs.

I disagree with Daniel Callahan's suggestion that limits be set on the resources made available for those who have reached an arbitrary age (because they have allegedly reached what he calls a "natural life span") but my disagreement is not the question here. I am concerned here with the book's contention that such limits can be "fixed in space" by stopping all research (or at least, what amounts to the same thing, stopping the funding for such research) aimed at extending such a limit. Even when limits on meeting second-order needs must be set (and I am quite unwilling to grant that this must be done as long as available resources are wasted and as long as extreme luxuries for some continue at the very time that limiting access for others to second-order necessities is sought), setting limits on attempts to extend such limits is morally illegitimate. When we arbitrarily limit the consumer base (say, by not treating the aged after a certain age) and deny the validity of experimentation to extend it (say, by not funding experimentation aimed at extending the useful lifespan), we infringe upon second-order needs. Health care (and, at times, education) are as necessary for a successful, ripe, and prosperous old age as they are for a vigorous youth. Saying that experiments to extend the consumer base have no validity cuts off life at a time when many of the lives cut off could be—and oftentimes are—successful and happy ones.

So that limits on some activities may be set while a search for extending such limits continues, a notion of what is and what is not experimental must be held clearly in mind. I would suggest that, especially when it comes to dealing with basic necessities, (1) limits need to be empirically determined; (2) we acknowledge the temporal nature of such limits; (3) we recognize an intermediate experimental step between the limit today and the expansion of such limits tomorrow; and (4) we periodically reexamine and re-set the limits in accordance with new conditions and knowledge developed by further thought and experimentation. For that reason, it seems reasonable that we fund only those procedures and interventions within the framework of our current limits, and that we rigidly control (and fund) the intermediate experimental step so that experimentation is not carried on under the guise of therapy and so that experimentation occurs only in fully understood, voluntary, and controlled situations. Such a way of proceeding is not confined to medicine: Education, likewise, has its practical (therapeutic) and its tentatively innovative (experimental) side. Setting limits on experimentation to extend limits (whether limits are set on experimenting with limited resources or with stretching the consumer base) forecloses the future. There is, however, an often difficult-to-determine point at which innovation and experimentation blend into legitimate and eventually established practice. What is evidently experimental and what clearly therapeutic is not usually difficult to determine: Operating expanding abdominal aneurysms or giving penicillin to patients with streptococcal endocarditis is clearly therapeutic; the long-term use of the artificial heart is clearly experimental. We say that the one is clearly therapeutic because a previously agreed-to track record has been established and that the other is experimental because such an agreed-upon track record is lacking. We can, within an acceptable margin of error, predict the long- and short-term outcome of one while we cannot do so for the other.

Research and practice (experimentation and intervention) are, as Thomasma has pointed out, "logically distinct activities."[6] Experimentation or research is designed to produce knowledge and information about a specific topic either for its own sake ("pure science," as when a scientist seeks to find out more about the way enzymes function) or to be better able to address a specific practical problem (as when a researcher tries to find a chemotherapeutic regimen to deal more effectively with lung cancer). I am not by any means implying that the fruits of investigation in pure science are not at least as important or as practically useful as are those dealing with more immediately concrete matters. On the contrary: Without advances in pure science, applied science soon withers. Experimentation is a forging into the more-or-less unknown; unknown because the outcome, by the very nature of the activity, is not even statistically predictable. When research is carried on in clinical medicine, this means that those participating as subjects of such research can have no clear idea whether they stand to benefit or, perhaps, lose by the venture. At times, as when they are fatally ill, they may have nothing or little to lose and, therefore, may be more than eager to participate. Nevertheless, the primary purpose of the experiment is to "produce generalizable knowledge" rather than to benefit individual patients.[6] Individual patients may benefit from such a venture but that is neither predictable (if it were it would not be experimental) nor can it be the primary focus of the investigation. (This quandary sets up a number of difficult dilemmas for research workers who are simultaneously engaged in treating and in experimenting on individual patients. Such ethical dilemmas are of great importance but are not directly pertinent to this discussion).

Similar considerations concern experimentation in the field of education. Radical changes in method or content designed to produce better results need to be tried experimentally and evaluated before being generalized. Experimentation here likewise seeks generalizable knowledge which can be applied to serve the individual good only after it has been properly evaluated. Applying a new idea wholesale and "therapeutically" before it has been properly tried under experimental conditions is bad experimentation and irresponsible practice in medicine as well as in education.

The outcome of today's experiment is intended to be tomorrow's therapy. On the other hand, the subject of the experiment may be found wanting or even detrimental and, therefore, not be applicable to the clinical practice of either medicine or education. Just as the activity of experimentation and therapeusis must be held logically separate, the limits set on either and the funding supplied for their pursuit must be logically separate. Setting limits on today's practice, on what funds should be made available for treating patients is quite a different thing from setting limits on experimentation, the outcome of which determines future practice.

An example taken from medicine (one can easily think of example from education) may serve:

> I was involved in a decision about an infant born with kidney disease. The child was suffering from a condition in which vast quantities of serum proteins were lost in the urine, a condition which when congenital is, as far as is known, irreversible and rapidly fatal. The only hope seemed to be the removal of the infant's kidneys. This was done and the child was henceforth maintained on dialysis. After several months it was decided that the child had attained sufficient size to receive a kidney transplant. By that time significant impairments not only of growth and development but also of cognitive development had occurred. Chances were that, even should the child live, she would never be mentally normal. The father volunteered as donor and was, ultimately, accepted.

> There are, of course, several ethical problems here. I will ignore all but one. Transplanting organs into a person requires suppression of that person's immune system. To the best of our knowledge, this must be maintained, to a greater or lesser degree, for a very long time if not for life. It involves, among other things, the administration of steroids which are known to have a profound effect on metabolism and, therefore, on muscle, bone, endocrine, and other structures. We have a good idea of what happens to adults and to some older children maintained on such drugs. The results, while hardly desirable or pleasant, are usually acceptable—at least in view of the alternative. Organ transplantation in infants and long term immunosupression in infants lacks a track record: We have really no idea what the results are or might be. Transplanting organs into infants—today and by almost everyone's definition—is experimental.

Transplanting organs into infants can be framed as therapeutic ("the infant might benefit") or it can be viewed experimentally ("we really don't know what might happen to the child). Framing a thing or procedure as experimental or as therapeutic has a number of inevitable consequences. It determines: (1) not only how we will present the problem to patient and community but also what patients will decide to do; (2) whether we feel obligated to follow a rigorous protocol aimed at extracting as much information as possible so that a track record can be established or whether we feel obligated to individualize treatment; (3) the locus of operation (experiments done under rigorous protocol are performed at preestablished centers); and (4) the source of the monetary support for such a venture. Will the patient pay? the patient's insurance company? will the community pay from funds set aside for patient care? or will support come from research grants or communal sources specifically earmarked for research? (After all, patients or those paying the bill for them ought not to be expected to pay the bill for allowing themselves to be experimental objects).

When allocating resources, one may easily decide that since no track record exists, this procedure is experimental, and, therefore, that: (1) emphasis to the parents must be placed on the fact that we are mainly gathering information rather than benefiting their child (we hope for benefit but can provide few guidelines as to outcome); (2) we are committed to following a rigorous protocol; (3) we may have to refer the patient to an appropriate and possibly inconvenient location; and (4) we will not be able to bill the patient or insurance company but will have to rely on research grants or other research sources. Such a decision has profound implications for the patient, for the professional, and for the community. A community may decide to set its limits and not fund such questionably therapeutic interventions while continuing to try to "stretch the limits" for such patients by allowing (and funding) experimentation done under proper circumstances.

I want to spend a little time contrasting the notions of experimentation with those of therapeusis in order to show that limits set on one do not necessarily or legitimately entail limits on the other. When we limit the application of some method, procedure, or drug (be it in medicine or in education), when, in other words, we set limits to therapeusis in its broadest sense, we limit what can be done in the present. This does not entail setting limits on the future. It merely says that under existing circumstances (scientific as well as social) a given method, procedure, or drug is not acceptable for general application, perhaps because it is considered unproven or dangerous. Or it may be the case that a given method, drug, or procedure is safe and useful but is so incredibly expensive that it wastes resources needed more desperately elsewhere. The decision that a method, drug, or procedure does not have sufficiently proven merit is one properly delegated to experts in the field. It is largely a scientific decision made by appropriate experts (be they scientists, physicians, or educators) and constitutes the setting of professional limits. The decision that a proven method, drug, or procedure is simply too expensive is more properly made by those nonexperts delegated by the community to make such decisions. Here experts may properly act as advisers, establishing a framework of current and probable future usefulness, but the decision itself is much more a social one and constitutes the setting of social limits.

When, however, we stop experimentation at the borders of the limits (whether they are scientific limits or social ones) we limit not only present activity but in a very real sense preclude the future. Such a decision needs far more justification than the decision not to apply a given modality at a given time. A decision of this sort locks us into the present and forecloses options. Occasionally this may seem justified: stopping certain experiments aimed at developing extremely virulent and hardy microorganisms or stopping the development of nuclear weapons may be examples. But such examples are properly rare. Setting limits to expanding our knowledge is a form of censorship with all the odious and dangerous overtones and consequences that censorship has. Further, communities may well decide to set priorities by stopping funding for the refinement of luxury when more important needs go begging. Those things envisioned by the community as legitimate first- or second-order necessities have a different standing than do luxury items. Stopping (or stopping the funding) of experimentation aimed at what society considers to be purely destructive or what communities consider to be purely luxury items is a far different matter than stopping research aimed at expanding access to life or access to those things in life which make it worthwhile.

The often very large gray zone between what we consider to be therapeutic and what we consider to be experimental should not discourage us from seeking to delineate these concepts. The statements that what is well established as useful is therapeutic and that what is of questionable or tentative value is experimental are true as far as they go, but they do not, in fact, go very far. Discernment of what is well established as well as what is questionable or tentative demands a framework of values. Experts may help in constructing such a framework: They may point out scientific justification for a particular choice and provide data legitimizing their contention. But experts cannot establish the values in which such a decision is framed.

Criteria for what we call "proof" (i.e., what we consider to be established) as well as what we consider to be "sufficient" proof to move from the experimental to the therapeutic) are socially constructed and determined. They are far from absolute. Today's criteria (and with them today's proof) may be wrong tomorrow, and what is considered sufficient in one setting or context may not be in another. Allowing the use of a drug or procedure for a condition, for which no alternative course is open, is a far different matter than allowing the use of a procedure or drug when working alternatives are available. When we say that giving penicillin or operating aneurysms is therapeutic, we imply that the socially set criteria of usefulness have been met, whereas, for the use of artificial hearts on a long-term basis, they have not. Likewise the decision that acceptable alternative courses are open depends ultimately on socially determined criteria. The crux of the matter, then, is the setting of criteria within a social framework.

When innovative methods of therapy (be it in medicine or education) are prematurely released and applied, a large amount of mischief may follow. When the release of innovative methods of therapy are unduly delayed, unnecessary suffering may result. Criteria for determining what is experimental and what is therapeutic need to be set with goals in mind. For example, consider the case of a drug for the treatment of a fatal illness for which no good treatment is available: The change in at drug's status, from experimental to therapeutic, should be more rapidly accomplished than the release of an alternative drug for the treatment of a condition for which good treatment is already available.

When one speaks of an experimental procedure, drug, or method one is speaking about a procedure, drug, or method which lacks a proper track record. To establish whether it has merit, what the side effects are, and what the bad or disastrous consequences may be, criteria for testing under rigorously controlled circumstances need to be applied. Moving prematurely from the unknown to the accepted is not only risky business, it also means that we may never know the true merit or applicability of such a procedure, drug, or method, or that we may find out about it only after vast damage has been done. Medicine, as well as education, offers examples. In medicine some procedures or drugs that have traditionally been used lack experimental backing for their application and are used in ways which are, at best, questionable. The same can be said for education: Innovative programs (I think here of the craze for the "new math" or the "new reading" in the '60s) that are rushed into general practice before adequate testing may have disastrous results. Such bad experiences do not militate against innovation, but they suggest that the boundary between what is an experimental and what is properly a therapeutic method has to be carefully drawn and thoughtfully attended to. Decisions of this sort are decisions communities must carefully make and carefully adhere to.

We live in a world of finite resources but with enormous needs. We also live in a world in which the opportunities for meeting such needs and enriching the lives of all is greater than it has ever been. To accomplish our task, to help those today in need and to widen our ability to help others tomorrow, we must be the proper stewards of what we have. Being a proper steward requires more than husbanding today's resources: Where possible it implies investing in tomorrow so that resources can either be expanded or more efficiently used. Husbanding our resources today includes not wasting them on things of unproven or doubtful value, but it does not mean deciding now whether such things do or do not have such future value. When it comes to providing first-order necessities to all (or to experimenting with methods of meeting such needs better or for more people) the setting of limits is extremely problematic. Providing such necessities today for all who can profit from them is the first order of business of a just society accepting beneficent obligations; experimenting with better methods or with wider bases is a close second. Second-order necessities do not come far behind. As long as resources are available, limiting either first- or second-order necessities while allowing free access to luxuries for some promotes suffering and shatters solidarity.

## References

1. Kant I: *Kritik der Reinen Vernunft*. Baden-Baden: Suhrkamp Verlag, 1988.

2. Callahan D: *Setting Limits: Medical Goals in an Aging Society*. New York: Simon & Schuster, 1987.

3. Callahan D: *Health and the Good Society*. New York: Simon & Schuster, 1990.

4. Kant I: *Grundlegung zur Metaphysik der Sitten*. Baden-Baden: Suhrkamp Verlag, 1988.

5. Hardin G: The Tragedy of the Commons. *Science 162*:1243-48, 1968.

6. Thomasma DC: Applying General Medical Knowledge to Individuals: A Philosophical Analysis. *Theoret Med 9*:187-200, 1988.

# Chapter Seven

# Allocating Resources and Treating
# Individuals Fairly

So far I have sketched an ethic based on the capacity for suffering shared by all sentient beings and have advanced the claim that such a capacity offers an at least prima facie protection to all such beings. It is an entity's capacity to suffer which grounds every other moral agent's prima facie obligation not to bring capricious harm to such entities. I have further claimed that our sense of obligation originates with our inherent sense of compassion and, furthermore, that the way we see our obligations has a great deal to do with our sense of community. Both compassion and the belief that beneficence has moral force firmly grounds an obligation not only to refrain from causing but, where possible, to ameliorate suffering. To accomplish this task, I have examined some of the ways of grounding communities in a variety of notions of social contract and argued for a social contract not based on fear, terror, or even trust but rather have argued for a social contract grounded in the necessary biosocial fact of the individual's nurture within family or group. Infants develop their realization of self and, eventually, their fledgling autonomy in the embrace of a nurturing environment. Trust, and eventually fear and terror, develop in such an environment. If this is true, then experiencing beneficence ontologically precedes the development of autonomy, and beneficent obligations are at least as necessary in the human community as is respect for autonomy. Beyond this, I have tried to sketch an interrelationship not only of individuals and their particular communities but also the interrelationship among communities and, ultimately, the relationship of all such communities with their greater worldwide family.

Communities built on a beneficent model are obligated to do far more than merely refrain from causing suffering and must do far more than merely refrain from preventing access to the good things of life. If communities built on a beneficent model take their obligations seriously, such communities must become actively involved in ameliorating the suffering of their members as well as with facilitating the access of all their members to a fair opportunity range. Persons denied a fair opportunity range and frustrated in their attempts to lead the kind of life to which their talents and energies would otherwise entitle them inevitably suffer.

Communities depend on solidarity to develop and endure. In turn, a sense of solidarity with one another necessitates the feeling that all of us are concerned with each other's suffering and wellbeing. Concern for each other's welfare, as much as respect for each other's autonomy and the knowledge that both these feelings pervade community, are essential if a sense of solidarity is to flourish. The knowledge that the community will look with equanimity upon our suffering, the knowledge that the powerful will continue to have every right to enforce their power regardless of the wellbeing of others eventually shatters solidarity and ruptures community even when we know that our individual autonomy will be respected. The lessons of history should be ample proof for such a statement.

There is an almost inevitable conflict between the interest an individual has in protecting her own autonomy and the interests communities have in fostering communal interests. Likewise, the virtues of private and communal relationships are often seen as opposed virtues, the one having much more to do with what Stuart Hampshire calls "a fastidious sense of honor" and the other with what he terms "largeness of design."[1] He sees if not a resolution then a hope for mutual understanding in the inevitable deliberative process that any society or individual solving a problem must engage in. It is the presence and fairness of the process which ultimately makes it possible to speak of ethical commitment. The sometimes divergent virtues of "fastidious honor" and of "largeness of design" both have their place, but even having acknowledged that, adjudication between the inevitable clashes still remains difficult. I do not wish to suggest that such an adjudication is always possible nor that a perfect and complete system of morality can ever be elaborated. On the contrary: While I believe, as Stuart Hampshire suggests, that conflict is inevitable, I nevertheless believe that consensus or at least consensus in dealing with specific problems at specific times, can be reached by what he calls "rationally controlled hostility."[1] Such rationally controlled hostility may, in fact, be another way of looking at the dialectic and at the relationship between the interests and virtues of individual association and the interests and virtues of communal living.

What keeps rationally controlled hostility from eventuating in open warfare, and what keeps a dialectic operating peacefully, is, of course, the presence of fair process. Using the capacity for suffering and a notion that community originates in nurture as a framework for the "rationality" as well as the process of this conflict may help in dealing with some of the problems.

When communities decide how to spend communal funds for the common good, when, in other words, they get down to allocating resources, communities based on an ethic richer than a mere autonomy ethic will have to make decisions based on some notion of individual and communal needs. I have suggested that a way of looking at the concept of needs may be provided by looking at basic necessities as being either biologically necessary to sustain existence itself or socially necessary to create those conditions which make existence worth living. Basic necessities, then, are underpinned either by biological realities (first-order necessities) or by social factors (second-order necessities). The former are not generally variable: All creatures need air, food, water, warmth, and shelter if they are to survive. Second-order necessities, however, are variable depending on the social circumstances of a given time and place. They include those things required to sustain acceptable life within a given social context so that reasonable individual goals can be met. Such things serve to provide individuals with access to "a normal opportunity range which reasonable persons are likely to construct for themselves."[2] What can be considered to be a "normal opportunity range" and who can be considered to be "reasonable persons," are decisions made in community and are variable with time, place, and circumstance. I have argued that in modern industrialized societies such second-order necessities invariably must include education and health care. Attaining our society's fair opportunity range is not possible for people denied access to either. In a community based on a more-than-minimal ethic, furthermore, having access is defined not merely as having a clear path but likewise as having one's fair opportunities facilitated.

In deciding how to spend communal funds, limits on spending inevitably must be set. If resources were infinite and readily available to all for the asking, the question of allocating would never come up. Since, however, resources are ultimately finite, setting limits or rationing is necessary. I have suggested that setting limits on what may be available for consumption or use today is quite a different thing from setting limits on our trying to find ways to improve our ability to consume or use the things we have tomorrow. In looking at the whole notion of limits, a notion critical to the idea of allocation, we can either look at such limits as natural—set for us and, therefore, inevitable and immutable—or we can decide that limits are socially determined and, therefore, ours to construct and change. If one conceives of limits as natural, then setting limits (unless they are to be set below the natural limits) makes no sense: Limits have been set for us already and we must merely discover them. Once discovered, trying to stretch natural limits makes sense only if we look at nature as something manipulable and able to be turned to our benefit. Such limits then are not in fact ultimate limits but are changeable. Changeable limits, however, are not what those intent on having us recognize or set limits are, in fact, after. The claim that, ultimately, limits are natural, however, still says nothing about our capacity to discover what these limits are. To make such a discovery, even were we to believe that it could be made, we must rely either on a form of revelation or upon experimentation the results of which are true or false only within a socially predetermined context. Further, it is unclear why the naturalness in limits should matter. After all, natural conditions have never been seen as anything but opportunities to learn more so that, ultimately, yesterday's limit is no longer a limit tomorrow.

Setting limits on the spending of communal funds for the common good, either because what is sought is too expensive or because what is sought is unproven, are two different matters. The decision that a given activity is too expensive to be funded by the community is a decision socially arrived at; the decision that something is or is not proven is a decision made by persons socially acknowledged to be experts in a particular field. The criteria, however, for what does and what does not constitute acceptable proof are also largely a social construct, even if a social construct made with significant input by the experts themselves. Decisions that limits should not be explored or that limits should, if possible, not be stretched is quite another matter. I have argued that foreclosing such testing of limits forecloses the future and that it is an activity which should be foreclosed, if ever, only with the most extreme hesitancy and caution.

This chapter will try to deal with a few of the practical issues that follow from such considerations. The allocation of medical resources will be used as an example, but the chapter is not meant to confine its attention to medicine alone. Rather I am groping for a resolution between the problems seen in adjudicating between the justified claims of the individual for his liberty and freedom of action and the equally justified needs of the community. A resolution of this problem for all time is not possible: Times, conditions and with it values change and each community must forge its new standards and decisions from and through the old. What I am after is not a resolution applicable to all times but rather framework in which resolutions applicable to a given context can be sought.

As a starting point I shall advance the claim that neither a capitalist system—in which the needs of the community are given short shrift and the individual needs of the poor and powerless go begging—nor a Bolshevik-style communism—in which the community reigns supreme and the individual, while not in need, nevertheless is powerless and has little opportunity to flourish—is a system many of us would choose to be born into. Such a claim rests upon initial choice, a choice somewhat akin to the one Rawls suggests.[3] In essence, Rawls poses choice as something done behind "a veil of ignorance": a veil which does not permit us to see our particular situation of prosperity, health, or power but which sketches the general landscape in which we must choose. The considerations of the veil's thickness or the various other supposed defects associated with this theory are important but are not our concern here. Rawls' model, for our purposes, has evident heuristic power and will be used merely in that sense. If confronted with a choice between a life of unknown social station in the "social justice" of a Bolshevik-style communism or in the "individual liberty" and "opportunity" of capitalism, few of us could do more than shrug our shoulders or flip a coin. For many of us it might be a choice between, on the one hand, starving on the street with a full opportunity for speaking, publishing, and assembling freely and, on the other hand, having a full belly but unable to realize any of our potential or carry any of our hopes into fruition.

Many will claim that when I speak of Bolshevik-style communism, I really mean socialism. I do not. True socialism and what has recently passed for communism are related to each other as a pleasantly hot bath is related to a boiling cauldron: Both can be said to be warm but that is where the similarity ends. Socialism, quite distinct from Bolshevik-style communism, presupposes a community established to assure and support the flourishing of all its members to the full extent possible within communal resources and personal talents; it stands ready to limit some personal liberties by democratic process (the liberty to earn vast sums of money, for example) but it does so cautiously and only to meet what it, as a community, acknowledges to be the legitimate aspirations of all individuals. Limiting personal liberties is done in pursuit of agreed-upon values and goals beyond those of any single individual and in support of the community, which has a free-standing value of its own. While Bolshevik-style communism may pay lip service to such a vision, reality has taught us that lip service is as far as it goes.

Socialism as it is practiced in a variety of places (the Scandinavian countries are examples) is an evolving construct forged by people willing to cooperate and to help each other's flourishing, people whose vision of the good life includes a life lived in community rather than one lived in uncaring isolation. Communism practiced as Bolshevism, no less than capitalism, is concerned with maintaining the power structure of the state. Maintaining the power of the state is done not in pursuit of communal values and goals or in order to help individuals flourish but is done to maintain the power of those in control.

There are some these days who maintain that socialism is dead. Such a claim rests on the fact that the crass communism as practiced lately behind the iron curtain has discredited itself as a viable system. In the past, communism has advanced the claim that it *is* socialism, a claim which has been gladly taken up in the United States. The reason why the United States has embraced this claim is not just sheer ignorance of what socialism is, although there is certainly that. It is a convenient claim, for if such a claim were accepted it would discredit socialism, which capitalism properly sees as a much more threatening rival than communism is or ever has been. Communism as practiced behind the iron curtain was perhaps a military but never a severe ideological threat: The system was too empty, too repressive, and too inflexible to appeal to reflective people for any length of time. Socialism, however, is a much more serious rival: Socialism promises to all individuals not only social justice but also, while maintaining democratic control over the direction and evolution of society, offers individuals the ability to flourish. That indeed is a threat to the capitalist system, a system which leaves some few with incredible wealth, many in abject poverty and most in a precarious state in which their comfortable livelihood today may disappear and find them in poverty tomorrow. Above all, capitalism perpetually leaves those who are comfortably well off and compassionate and who subscribe to an at-least-partially beneficent ethic feeling vaguely guilty.

Allocating resources so that the hungry no longer go hungry, the homeless have shelter, and so that all have full access to educational opportunities and to basic health care requires an allocator. I have suggested that, ultimately, it is the community which must set the framework in which specific decisions can be made. In a practical sense, however, the community as allocator is a vague concept which needs fleshing out. Communities in meeting their responsibilities in this regard, cannot in practical terms act as a single body making such diverse decisions. The notion of communities acting presupposes an informed, educated, and caring electorate which has sufficient trust in the goodwill of others (and has sufficient historical reason to be trust-ing) to delegate the specifics to selected members. Even the most honest and trustworthy delegates, however, will need the advice of experts in the various fields to help them think through general as well as specific problems and to come up with general as well as, ultimately, with spe-cific answers. Thus communities must be engaged in a dialogue with their thinkers, its social philosophers and others who are privy to a needed body of knowledge and understanding, as well as with its more technically oriented experts. The community must trust these experts to come up with an honest assessment of the situation and to give their advice freely and without undue self-interest. Such experts, on the other hand, must have sufficient trust in the community to allow it to make ultimate choices, choosing, from among often disparate opinions and points of view, the particular point of view which seems most fruitful at that moment in time. Such a concept, basically a thumbnail sketch of the democratic process, can only operate successfully when all members of the community have had a fair opportunity to develop their abilities and skills. This is necessary not only so that they, as individuals, may flourish but because doing so underwrites the function of community itself. It is what having community as a value in itself is all about. Before allocation can take place effectively, wasting resources must be kept to a minimum. What constitutes waste, likewise, is a communal judgment expressed eventually in law and usage.

Education as well as medical care, in our society as in all modern societies, is a second-order necessity, that is, it is needed to assure to all members of a just community access to a fair opportunity range.[2] In almost all nations but the United States, at least basic health care is pro-vided to all members of the community regardless of their ability to pay. The details of how this is implemented vary from nation to nation: Some supply the same care for all, some have a two-tiered system and some supply free health care only to persons below a certain income range. In all nations, including in the United States, basic education is likewise supplied to all.

There is an analogy between a two-tiered educational and a two-tiered health care system. While virtually all nations, at least all non-third world nations, provide basic education without cost, and while many nations not only provide full educational opportunity to all but even provide a stipend to students so that they can live, many other nations—along with the United States—have adopted a basically two-tiered approach. Such an approach purports to provide basic schooling through high school but offers richer or further educational opportuni-ties either to those who can afford them or to those lucky enough to have outstanding talents. Furthermore, even those whose native talent is exceptional may have a very difficult time competing against those from wealthier homes whose talents, while comparatively mediocre, have had a better opportunity to be developed. As a result many would-be students are left with talents undeveloped and with aspirations unrealized. This two-tiered approach, evident even at lower levels, is instrumental in denying opportunity and frustrating talent. The wealthy can send their children to private schools far different than the schools the less wealthy can afford, and affluent school districts are apt to provide a quite different educational opportunity in their schools than do neighboring poorer districts.

The problem in American health care today is not even one of a two-tiered system. Those unable to afford health care (whether through private funds, insurance, or Medicaid) may well go without it. Charity clinics are few and far between and may not be accessible to those in need. People whose employment does not entail insurance benefits and who cannot afford either to buy insurance or to pay for their own care frequently go without. Rationing health care by ability to pay is a reality in America today. In remedying this situation, a variety of approaches, including a two tiered approach, have been proposed. Similar to what is the case in education, one has the choice of either providing complete care to all (and decide what level of care would be available for all) or of providing basic care and allowing those who desire more to purchase it for themselves.

On the surface both of these systems have merit: defining what will and what will not be considered under the rubric "health care" and then making it available to all who may need it is supported by the notion of equity; providing basic care and allowing those who may want to buy more to do so, is supported by the notion of respect for autonomy. Which system a community will choose, provided it has the resources to choose at all, will depend upon the way the community envisions its obligation. In other words, the particular choice will depend upon the way in which the dialectic tension between communal and individual interests has played out in a particular community: how reason has been used to control hostility.[1]

When communities use the concept of suffering as a basis for ethical decision making and ask which of their actions would tend to minimize the suffering of individuals within them, they will have to examine the issue squarely. If communities see their obligation as largely not causing suffering, they will act quite differently than they would if they saw their obligation as one of ameliorating it where possible. Those who have access to basic health care but are denied access to more complicated health care (dialysis or transplantation of organs) may suffer greatly from this knowledge. If, on the other hand, dialysis and transplantation is made available to no one (or, at least, if it is distributed by other than market forces) the suffering of all will be equal. Such decisions are decisions communities must make for themselves in full realization of their total resources and in full appreciation of the values which cause them to support one or the other enterprise.

Allocation takes place at several levels: first at the level of the largest allocating community, perhaps the state, which must allocate to the various enterprises it recognizes as being legitimate recipients of allocation. States, therefore, will have to decide how much to spend for defense, how much for education, how much for health care, how much for promoting the arts, and how much for myriad other enterprises. There is, at this level, a tension among lobbyists for each enterprise within the community demanding as much as they can possible receive for it. At the next level, the specific enterprise which has been allocated a certain amount must allocate whatever it has received to its constituent parts. Education, for example, must allocate to Head Start, or to the support of primary or of higher education; health care must allocate to public health, research, hospitals, etc. In turn, the component parts within the system now must allocate whatever resources they have been able to obtain to their individual sections. Hospitals, for example, must decide how much to allocate for transplant programs, birthing units, or outpatient departments. Things are, however, hardly that simple or, for that matter, unidirectional. At all levels, there is appeal to the higher allocator for more funds and a brisk competition among the various interests ensues. To allow fair allocation, "rationally controlled hostility" with its rationality based on reasonable and fair process is, of course, essential.

Communities may decide that transplantation, dialysis, or other more or less exotic technologies are too expensive to be given to certain population groups (say welfare recipients) and that the community would profit more by supporting immunization programs or basic health care for all. Such a decision depends on available resources as well as on values: When communities limit funds available for health care for welfare recipients (as, of course, they must, the question is not the limitation of funds but the extent of such a limitation) they force the agencies responsible for allocating such funds to make difficult choices. Only a certain amount is available and that amount, inevitably, must be spent to give essential services to as many as possible. If we object to limiting transplants for welfare recipients in order to give basic health care to others, we are saying either that (1) transplanting a few persons and consequently saving their lives has a greater value than giving basic health care, which is often largely preventive, to many others, or (2) we are simply expressing our frustration that both cannot be done with the funds available. If, in fact, the funds available do not permit both things to be done, a choice has to be made despite serious objections. But things do not end here. If we agree that, on the balance, giving basic and preventive health care to many is a wiser choice (is, in other words, a "larger design") but still find that doing so affronts our "fastidious sense of honour" we have an obligation to appeal to a higher allocator for more funds. In turn, the higher allocator has to make very similar choices and must, when these seem unduly harsh, appeal up to the next level of allocation. At the level at which decisions are made among the larger enterprises within the community (for example, choices between how much to give to defense and how much to education), these various appeals find the place where rational hostility can help adjudicate among these conflicting claims. It is here that a concept of community and the grounding of morality on the capacity of all members of the community to suffer may well be helpful. Can suffering be minimized by building a missile or by educating the young? Is, all things considered, lesser suffering likely if more are given access to a college education or access to exotic but individually highly effective medical interventions? The process of making such decisions, inevitably, takes place in a political framework.

Beyond the problem of allocating for health care needed today, the problem of allocating for research cannot be ignored. Research is done so that knowledge can be developed and, ultimately, a better tomorrow can be hoped for. It may well be the case that certain medical (or social) interventions cannot be made available to all but that, in order to have a better tomorrow, such interventions could be used within the framework of rigorously controlled experimentation. Here the intent is not to benefit individuals (indeed, whether they will or will not benefit is largely unknown and this lack of knowledge is what legitimates the experiment) but to benefit future others. The two activities, therapeusis and experimentation, need to be carefully separated in dealing with allocation issues.

The suggestion is often made that, in the medical arena of distribution, physicians act as gatekeepers, charged not only with seeking their patients' best interests but, simultaneously, charged with saving the community's resources. It is, in fact, the sort of thing which takes place in England when physicians are known to fail to offer dialysis to patients above a certain age by framing such denial as "being not medically indicated."[4] It is argued that physicians are, from a technical point of view and by virtue of their being on the scene, best equipped to make such decisions. Their special knowledge of the problem as well as their special knowledge of the specifics of each case surely would entitle them to make such decisions![5] On the other hand, others have argued that when physicians have a fair chance of serving their patients interests they cannot, within the current vision of the physician-patient relationship, very well allow considerations of costs, societal considerations or even the needs of others to sway their decision.[6,7] Expecting physicians to be gatekeepers, while simultaneously expecting them to live up to the rigorous standards of what is today understood to constitute ethical patient care, imposes conflicting values on an already confused profession.[8] When it comes to patient care, physicians are supposed to live up to a "fastidious sense of honor;" such a sense of honor clashes directly with their gatekeeper function.

Furthermore, having physicians act as gatekeepers moves the necessary social arena in which the tension between communal and individual interests is played out to the heart and head of one physician. It reduced the process of rational hostility to a conflict within one person who may herself have idiosyncratic rather than communally acceptable values and may, therefore, make what seem to be bizarre choices. Communities cannot simply delegate this responsibility to physicians without bringing about a major shift in the way in which traditional relationships are seen.

Having physicians act as gatekeepers in some instances is, of course, unavoidable. When it comes to allocating a single available heart to three patients who stand in need of a transplant, such decisions inevitably have to be made. When there are three persons in urgent need of a bed in the ICU and only one is available, a physician is in the likeliest position to choose. Even when, as I suggest, prior communal decisions should limit the choices individual physicians must make, areas of inevitable gatekeeping will appear. Holding such occurrences to a minimum and providing a previously agreed upon fair process for adjudicating such problems should go far in helping to alleviate the problem.

There is a complicated relationship between professionals and the communities which spawn them. To the detriment of both, this relationship is often not fully played out. On the one hand (as illustrated by the attempt to make professionals responsible for individual allocation issues) communities are tempted to hand such decisions to the professionals and to wash their hands of the problem: on the other hand, professionals often view their obligation within a purely individual framework in which they simply allocate available resources to individuals without examining issues beyond. Professionals legitimately have a role in advising communities about issues within their area of expertise, and communities legitimately must be concerned with enunciating values and with framing the rules and guidelines.

We have moved into an era in which both justice seen as predominantly and crassly autonomy-based and justice seen as predominantly and crassly beneficence-based have been found wanting. Bolshevik-style communism as well as American-style capitalism have failed in human terms. The opportunity to move beyond and to envision new horizons and prospects has opened up. Forging a new era is not only a possibility but has, indeed, become a necessity if civilization is to survive. Basing community on a vision which sees social contract as originating in nurture and, therefore, community as necessarily dedicated to the prevention and amelioration of suffering may provide a conceptual starting point for such an adventure.

## References

1. Hampshire S: *Innocence and Experience*. Cambridge: Harvard University Press, 1989.

2. Daniels N: *Just Health Care*. New York: Cambridge University Press, 1985.

3. Rawls J: *A Theory of Justice*. Cambridge: Harvard University Press, 1971.

4. Schwartz WB, Aaron HJ: *The Painful Prescription: Rationing Hospital Care*. Washington, DC: Brookings Institute, 1984.

5. Thurow L: Learning to Say "No." *NEJM 311*(24):1569-72, 1984.

6. Levinksy LN: The Doctor's Master. *NEJM 311*(24):1573-75, 1984.

7. Loewy EH: Costs Should Not Be a Factor in Medical Care. *NEJM 302*(12):607, 1980.

8. Churchill LR: *Rationing Health Care in America: Perceptions and Principles of Justice*. Notre Dame, IN: Notre Dame Press, 1987.

# Index

Nonmaleficence, community obligation, xi, 14
Nonvitalism, 44
Noumena, 101
Noxious stimuli, 7
Nozick, R., 62; and social contract, 65
Nurture, 72; as biological activity, 69; in communities, xi, 82; and development of autonomy, 77; effect on community, 73; and social contract, 72-73, 121; and social development, 69

Obedience, 30-31
Obligation: amelioration of suffering, xi; autonomy, 29; of beneficence, 29, 62, 63, 64; communal, xvii, 72, 121; and communal ethics, 55-56; definition of, 53; development of sense, 70; in feudal system, 58; and freedom, 53; to future, 72; and inclinations, 53-54; interpersonal, xiii; mutual, 57, 58; mutual nonharm, 61; nonmaleficence, xi, 14; perception of, 52-53; personal, xvii; prima facie, 14, 28-29, 32-33; relation to needs, 90; of respect, 74; roots, 55-56; and social contract, 67
Obligations: beneficence, 83, 87, 98, 99, 119; of beneficence, 66; communal, 82
*Odyssey* (Homer), 55
One tiered vs. two tiered, 127-128
Ontological priority, 57, 59-61, 74
Opportunity, access to, 94, 96, 99, 122, 123, 127; range, Daniels, 93

Pain as alarm, 6
Pain, relationship to suffering, 3, 4, 6-10, 11-12
Paternalism, 70; as extreme beneficence, 76, 77; and limits, 106
Pellegrino, E.D., 66; on autonomy, 71, 74

Perfect duties (Kantian), 62
Permanent vegetative state, 40, 44
Phenomena, 101
*Philoctetes* (Sophocles), xiii
Physicians; concepts of justice, ix; concepts of society, ix; as gatekeepers, 130-131; relationship to government, ix; role in resource allocation, 130-31
Pity, in primitive beings, x
Plato, 58; on social good, 55
Pleasure, 27
Pleasure principle, 4
Potentiality, 49, 50
Praiseworthiness, 41-42
Predetermination, 21
Prima facie obligation, 14, 28-29, 32-3
Primary moral worth, defined, 35-36; differences in 43-48, 54, 65
Principles, 21
Privacy, xv
Process (in conflict resolution), 122

Rainsborough, 58
Rationality, 19, 33
Rationalization, 42
Rawls, J., 31-32, 125
Reality, 18; ethical, 20, 21; physical, 20, 21
Reasoning, 19-20
Reductionism, xv
Reflection, in ethics, 70
Reflex, 68
Reflex behaviour, 57
Relativism: cultural, 18, 20, 24; socially determined, 109
Religion. *See* Theology
*Republic* (Plato), 58
Research. *See* Experimentation
Resolution of conflict, 122-123
Resources: allocation, xiv, xvii, 83, 90, 101, 104, 109, 116, 121-32; finite, 101, 105, 119, 123; relationship to needs, 119; waste, 127